HAUNTED
MYSTIC

HAUNTED MYSTIC

COURTNEY McINVALE

HAUNTED
America

Published by Haunted America
A Division of The History Press
Charleston, SC 29403
www.historypress.net

Back cover, inset: Photo from the Dickinson Collection, courtesy of the Mystic River Historical
Society, Inc., Mystic, Connecticut.

First published 2014

Manufactured in the United States

ISBN 978.1.62619.414.4

Library of Congress CIP data applied for.

Notice: The information in this book is true and complete to the best of our knowledge. It is
offered without guarantee on the part of the author or The History Press. The author and
The History Press disclaim all liability in connection with the use of this book.

This book is dedicated to my husband, Marty, who believes in my every venture and my writing talents with his whole heart. Marty provides such unwavering support in my life, and he has believed in this book from its first written word. He sees in me what I have never been able to and has instilled in me the confidence I needed to pursue my dreams of becoming a true author.

CONTENTS

ACKNOWLEDGEMENTS

It's truly amazing the amount of research, assistance and support that goes into the completion of any book. In fact, there is such an enormous scope of ground to cover that it would be next to impossible to do without the assistance, knowledge and support given by local historians, community members and, of course, beloved family friends.

I'd first like to extend my utmost gratitude and many thanks to Dorrie Hanna, president of the Mystic River Historical Society. Without her tremendous help in locating historic photos and finding a large plethora of unique Mystic history to read through, this book could never have happened. Dorrie happily listened to my lists of spooky buildings and tales and then ventured out to find the perfect photographs and detailed factoids of each, searching her archives for the most pertinent information. Dorrie's hours of research and assistance enabled *Haunted Mystic* to come alive. In the process, I was also able to enjoy lots of laughs and good conversation as we delved into local history together.

An enormous thanks must also be given to the New England Spiritual Team, Inc., and founder Michael Carroll. Their authenticity, reliability and enthusiasm for all things paranormal are a force to be reckoned with in the ghost hunting world. Through their generous sharing of stories, experiences and investigations, I was able to get a true sense of such a hair-raising haunt in Mystic and develop such lovely friends well known in the paranormal arena.

To Michael Cardillo Jr. and Robert Lecce Jr., I thank you for opening up your beautiful inn, sharing your photos and your history and bringing to life such a stunning piece of New England history within your property. Your hospitality and your conversation put a smile on my face and brought back all the good memories that come with being in a haunted home. This gave me such excitement for this book and for the telling of your stories.

Thanks also to Allie Nasin of the Captain Daniel Packer Inne. You made Ada and the captain come to life with your recounting of their numerous haunts and your openness to sharing the spooky yet fascinating sides of your establishment. You were the first confirmation for me that Mystic was the perfect place for a ghost tour and a haunted book. Allie, not only have you introduced me to the Mystic community, but your contributions also helped bring new light to Daniel Packer's colored past, successfully setting the wheels in motion for all my research into Mystic's ghostly past.

Debbie Gross, your tales of friendship and ghostly visits at two of Mystic's favorite haunts helped me to depict the deep-seated belief and knowledge that those we love and know in this life are always watching over us and, even more interestingly, that they never lose their sense of humor. Thank you for sharing your personal stories of such friendly spirits.

To the volunteers at Indian and Colonial Research Center (ICRC) and their fearless leader, Joan Kohn, your support from the moment I walked through your doors and told you about this book and my tours was astounding. The generous sharing of research materials was invaluable. Because of the folks at the ICRC, the Pequot War and the Mystic Massacre no longer remained words on a page in a history book but an event whose picture was so clearly painted for me in detail that I was able to gain the most incredible insight to the events that happened that fateful night of May 1637.

Anne Thacher, at Stonington Historical Society, I can't thank you enough for poring over maps over a century old trying to pinpoint exact locations and property owners with me. Your assistance in locating information for all my sites on the Stonington side of the river was astounding.

To the staff at the Voodoo Grill and Margherita's, thank you for sharing your ghostly tales and recounting for me your frightful experiences. Your experiences bring the veracity and the soul to this entire book.

Denny Kitchin and Jeff Fillback, what supportive friends and pseudo-brothers you have been. Thank God, I was able to have two English majors so close to me looking over my writing with no judgment passed, providing the necessary criticism any writer requires. What a phenomenal help you have been.

Finally, last but definitely not least, to my mom, my sisters and my husband, your patience with me as I have labored over these pages, come to you for guidance and pursued research on such an unconventional pursuit has been unbelievable. There are no words that could thank you enough. You all are the light of my life. Shelby, the photos you contributed are incredible, and your preliminary research helped me to hit the ground running. Savannah, your positive attitude and constant motivation keeps me going every day in doing what I love and reminded me to never abandon my love of writing. Mom, your support and bragging keeps me always striving to be the best I can be and reminds me what enormous love I have backing me in all my pursuits—no matter how strange they may be. And Marty, your constant, consistent reminders of what I'm capable of and your patience with me as I research and write remind me how proud you are of me and prove to me what a lucky gal I am. Without that emotional support, I may have never even attempted this pursuit.

INTRODUCTION

So many different parts of my life journey so far have led to the development of a book about the hauntings of Mystic Country. As a native of the Nutmeg State and a connoisseur of any and all literature involving history, my passion for local lore was established. This combination, thrown in with a lifelong dream to become an author, confirmed that the foundation had been set. I, Courtney McInvale, was well on my way to write a book set in authentic, antiquated New England.

A "haunted" book, however, would arise from a different journey. Penning the stories, tales and experiences of local paranormal phenomena was admittedly not where I initially saw my passion taking me and would require such a unique perspective.

I grew up in East Hampton, Connecticut, located in central Connecticut in a more rural area of Middlesex County. No particular landmarks or grand structures allow East Hampton to be pointed out on a map, but it's nestled quaintly off of Route 2 with some of its fellow rural communities and distant suburbs of Hartford and just down Route 66 from its larger neighbors of Middletown and Portland. Founded in 1739, East Hampton is no stranger to early English settlement and is one of the more historic smaller communities alive and well today in the Constitution State. Not quite the bustling metropolis many other towns have grown to be, the population increased to just around fourteen thousand people at the turn of the century. Many of these residents are in colonial or historic homes just a hop, skip and a jump away from the massive Lake Pocotopaug. East

Hampton is on the western end of what is now Eastern Connecticut, sitting a mere thirty-five-minute drive away from its southern neighbor of Mystic, the showcased locale of this book.

East Hampton is more than just a small town. It is also the home of the haunted house in which I was born and raised. I grew up as the eldest child with my two younger sisters in good ol' Belltown (East Hampton earned this nickname for housing one of the first and largest American bell factories, Bevin Bell). I had an extremely happy childhood and close-knit family, and our home was located in its own special piece of local history, directly across the street from the esteemed local Belltown legend Ms. Bevin herself.

Raised by our parents, a local police officer and a public school teacher, life couldn't be quainter. And for a long time it was just that. We knew our neighbors, we knew everyone in our school classes and our home was safe. We never had to lock a door, and Smalltown, USA maintained its romanticism. Life for us as children was full of homework, Little League, basketball leagues, student council meetings and all the things that define one's journey to adulthood. We raked leaves in the fall, jumping in giant piles of them before they were thrown into the jack-o-lantern-type bag display; planted gardens of flowers; built snowmen with friends; and sat on the porch with our parents, rocking on the giant swing. In all, we were living a small-town New England dream.

What many did not know, however, is that in that small, blue colonial on top of Summit Street, appliances were functioning on their own, doors opened and closed with no one present and urgent knocking sounds emitted from the walls in the dead of night. Footsteps creaked down the steps when no one in the family was utilizing them, strange aromas wafted through the house, beds shook, the wallpaper bled and mysterious figures made appearances at the bedsides of all of us who lived there. The happenings evolved as the years went on, affecting everyone in the household so very differently.

Eventually, the infamous Warren family whose name you may recognize from films and novels such as *The Conjuring* and *The Amityville Horror* was called upon by my mother in the early 2000s when I was just a teen. Lorraine Warren showed up with assistance from her team. Her husband, Ed, was ill and could not attend this particular investigation. Mrs. Warren and her son-in-law performed a cleansing and an exorcism of the house, concluding at the finish that the house was more than just a hotbed of paranormal activity. The house was also a spiritual portal to the other side, which allowed negative energies to enter in almost as easily as the harmless entities. Lorraine even surmised that some of these evil entities contributed to the mental decline of my father.

A well-known psychic and sensitive, Lorraine Warren informed my mother that both she and I possessed the ability to see and feel those who have departed. Essentially, on top of the home's propensity for spirit activity, we stood as lights in the darkness to any wandering souls looking for a home.

Though the cleansing assisted in reducing attacks by negative entities, the spiritual energies continued to roam the premises and cause inexplicable phenomena. By 2006, my mother sold the home, emotionally exhausted from the twenty years she had lived there and ready for a fresh start. Town hall records indicate that the house has changed hands four times since 2006, with all the subsequent residents citing paranormal experiences as the reason for their departure.

Perhaps fear, embarrassment or a strange combination of both hindered me, but in fact, it took years to accept the truth of my own past. The truth was that I had grown up haunted. It took even longer for me to become comfortable with the frequency with which unexplained spiritual occurrences had followed me throughout life. Even with that acknowledgement of things that I have seen, there was still this sort of stigma in society regarding those who believed in ghosts or even saw apparitions themselves. Time, support and sharing stories with those closest to me in my family and friends who had ghostly stories of their own helped me to see past that social stigma. Ultimately, I was able to learn that experiencing the paranormal and having sensitivity to seeing things that others cannot see did indeed set me apart from many of my fellow human beings, but it was in a very positive way. Others were interested to hear my story, and I was interested to find out more about this incredibly underexplored world of supernatural occurrences.

I embraced my experiences. They fit into a strange paradox of being both frightening and amazing, giving me that very unique perspective required to tell tales of the paranormal in a way that encompasses the truth of history and the spirits of those who walked the earth before us. By choosing to embrace my past and my sensitivities, I am now able to share with the world via writing and a local tour business how very alive history is today in the spirits that surround us.

After leaving the house for college, I lived in various parts of the East Coast and dabbled correspondingly with varying careers before I finally found myself looking back to home. New England was home. Connecticut

Mystic River Bascule Bridge (Drawbridge) view from Cottrell Street. *Photo by Shelby McInvale.*

was home. Knowledge of and experience with paranormal phenomena was my rare yet amazing asset to bring to my local community and to my writing.

When I began to study Connecticut lore, legends, history and ghostly sightings, it did not take long to become instantaneously attracted to Mystic Country. My studies in history, my intrigue with the supernatural and my inevitable adoration of both found new life in southeastern Connecticut.

When one thinks of Connecticut, he or she may think of oceans, changing seasons, fine dining, familiar mom-and-pop shops, nautical themes, deep forests, historic homesteads and an ambience allowing you to take a step back in time. While Connecticut as an entire entity encompasses these offerings throughout, Mystic, Connecticut, harbors the entire collection in its beautiful riverfront community. With no shortage of Connecticut history—dating as one of the first settlements in New England—it came as no wonder that ghost stories would abound in Mystic.

Set on the water—a natural conduit for spirit activity—history lives on in Mystic in the form of many a ghostly resident who still wanders through their old stomping grounds. Amid the photo-happy tourists, the delicious smells from the surrounding restaurants or the whistling bells and flashing lights of the local drawbridge, you just may catch a glimpse of a Civil War soldier or a man in a sea captain's attire standing at the corner or passing you on the street. If you do, don't be alarmed. Just smile and know that you got your very own taste of Haunted Mystic.

Chapter 1

THE BLOOD AND FIRE
THAT HAUNT THE LAND

DOWNTOWN MYSTIC

On especially quiet spring evenings as the moon has long since risen over Mystic Country, sitting high in the sky, and not too long before the sun begins to rise, you can hear the roar of fiery blazes, seemingly consuming the land. Amid the roar, there are the faint screams or suffering cries of what could only be throngs of people trying to escape. A swish of the wind causes you to look around and see which way the smoke is blowing. As you anxiously search for the source, almost dizzying yourself, you hear the tromping of feet down the hillside. Your hair stands on end. What is happening? Rubbing your eyes and blinking once or twice, you gather your emotions and gaze at your surroundings once more. Somehow, everything around you seems secure. There's the drawbridge over a quiet, tamed river; there's the shops closed down for the night, lit up only by glowing street lamps; and there are the quiet residents sitting in their colonial homes. Laughter fills the air from guests enjoying their final round of local brew at a nearby pub, and you realize that all is as it should be in downtown Mystic. Something happened though. You heard it. You felt it. You can't shake the feeling that there was a furious conflagration right behind you, with victims helplessly trapped within.

When one thinks of Mystic, one thinks of the beauty that it brings to Connecticut, the tales of the seafaring captains, the boutiques for a most exceptional shopping experience and restaurants full of exquisite dining. Mystic has a scenic drawbridge; the iconic Mystic Seaport, with accompanying antiquated ships to tour; and one of the most respected and renowned aquariums in the nation. All these things are true to the Mystic, Connecticut region of today and depict beautifully the beloved community that Mystic has developed into. Mystic is an authentic representation of quintessential New England.

That being said, one thing that often goes forgotten is that early Mystic's beginnings came as a result of one of the darkest pieces of American history. The emergence of Mystic came on the heels of a mass genocide. Mystic Country is home to the first massacre that ever occurred in what would become United States territory. Early America was a time of revolution, forging new terrain and trade relationships and separating from the monarchy of England. It was a time to establish democracy and develop a culture of its very own.

These brave new ventures did not come without sacrifice and war. Many of these initial battles on our soil were between the European settlers and those indigenous to the North American land. Some encounters resulted in violence and the horrendous slaughtering of the Native Americans. In the 1600s and even through to the early 1900s, many people believed that

Scenic Mystic Gravel Street and downtown view. *Photo by Shelby McInvale.*

the battles and wars that took place were necessary in the establishment of the nation, and the British soldiers and captains were held in high regard, revered for their accomplishments in conquering land across the East Coast and beyond. As our knowledge about what exactly transpired hundreds of years ago has risen in accord, a more rational assessment has taken place, concluding that the violent nature of these land-conquering expeditions was completely unnecessary.

The Native Americans, the first inhabitants of our country, were robbed of their land and their lives. The violence that took place in those early years was incomprehensible. While founding a new nation in Western civilization, some battles would prove to be inevitable and necessary, but oftentimes there were battle practices that no one today could possibly condone. They say war is hell, and to be sure, the Pequot War in Mystic was just that.

By the seventeenth century, the Pequot tribe inhabited a large part of the land around what is now known as the Mystic River. While there would have been multiple forts in the area, the largest fort was set apart on top of Pequot Hill. It was no more than a mile from the riverfront but in a safe, dry place due to its elevation. The Pequots were a respected yet feared tribe. Of all Native American tribes in the southern New England area, they were known to be some of the wealthiest and most skilled in the vicinity. In fact, among Native Americans throughout the land at the time, the Pequot tribe dominated on all fronts—economically, politically and with their "military."

Knowledge of the Pequots' well-trained warriors led to controversy among historians in regard to the exact derivation of the Pequot name. Some scholars claim that the name comes from the word *Pequttôog*, meaning "destroyers." Other specialists, including many modern members of the Pequot tribe, believe the term Pequot means the shallowness of a body of water, which could also ring true due to their tribe's proximity to the Long Island Sound and to the river itself. Regardless, legend of their ability and the fear they could invoke in battle was so profound that the name Pequot meaning destroyer became such a believable theory. (Additionally, the name Mystic, formerly called Mistick, was also inspired by the Pequots. The term *missi-tuk* described a large river whose waters are driven into waves by tides or wind.)

The indigenous Pequots were also great land cultivators in Connecticut and occupied a great deal of historic Connecticut land stretching between the Niantic River, the Wecapaugh River and the Narragansett River in what is now western Rhode Island. There were believed to be over sixteen thousand Pequots in the Connecticut River communities by the early 1600s. Other very close, local and neighboring tribes included the Mohegans and the Narragansetts.

As Western European (primarily the Dutch and British) settlers came over, with them came diseases to which Native Americans had no immunity. Several outbreaks scourged the New England area and all but decimated much of the Native American Indian populations. The smallpox epidemic of 1616 to 1619 was the first plague to kill many natives in New England. The Pequots remained virtually unscathed by this epidemic, but the epidemic that followed fourteen years later in 1633 took over 80 percent of the Pequots throughout the Mystic Country area. It is believed that, at most, three to four thousand Pequots were left by the year 1634.

Initially, the native relationship with the British was very amicable, despite the smallpox outbreaks. After the outbreaks, some areas or forts where the populations were completely taken by illness provided fertile ground and the colonial settlers actually moved in swiftly in order to utilize the land that had already been primed for cultivation and home building by the Native Americans. Up until the 1630s, trade agreements had been established between the settlers and Native Americans of all tribes. The Indians would receive different goods representative of the Western world and in turn exchange their highly valued wampum beads.

Despite these endeavors, tensions grew. The Native Americans were suffering from the aforementioned illnesses, and in the meantime, these new settlers—being the very religious, Christian English folk that they were—took close observation of their new neighbors' spiritual practices and societal structure with wary and disapproving eyes. The English interpreted wigwams and other native structures as inferior to the "real architecture" that they were familiar with, and above that, they believed the natives to be living in sin. They had, after all, witnessed them using what seemed to be supernatural powers by going into trances, utilizing tobacco in ritual and speaking of dreams as if they had control or meaning. Their worshipping practices took place outside and appeared barbaric. The newly arriving British concluded that the Native Americans were doing nothing more than communing with the devil. The natives worshipped and used nature and wilderness in everything they did. Respect of the land was of utmost importance to them since they knew that the land provided for them. The colonists saw wilderness as the devil and occupants of the wilderness as children of Satan. Combine these rituals with the natives' minimal dress and societal treatment of women as equals, and the British surmised that they were clearly living as heathens and had no regard for the true God. In sum, the English felt that the way the Indians treated their wives, practiced spiritual rituals and lived so closely to nature was despicable, and the settlers' feelings of wariness turned into spite. They felt scandalized and turned their shock into a hate that would come to dictate the massacre they planned in 1637 and would later boast proudly of.

Wanting to dispose of their neighbors once and for all, the English decided to approach the remaining Mystic natives in regard to taking the last Pequot fort. The English believed land could only be owned if it was tamed, thus the Pequots did not truly own land by their definition. They thought it would be an easy approach to retrieve the land that they desired. Pequots had previously maintained the control they had left by cooperating in trade agreements with the Dutch and English. When the English sent representatives to negotiate a land deal, the Pequots promptly refused. They, of course, had absolutely no interest in surrendering their land.

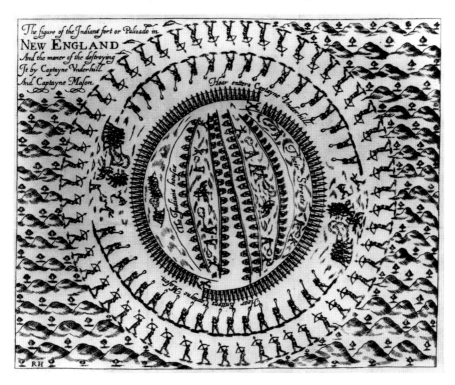

Pequot Fort depiction drawn in 1638. *Image courtesy of the Library of Congress.*

Sensing a more hostile motive behind the English approach, the Pequots sent raiding warriors against them, and as a result of these raiding parties came the death of an Englishman named John Olden. The Pequots had successfully sent their warning, and in retaliation, the British killed a few Pequot men. Ultimately, the Native Americans believed the roles were set in that both sides were dangerous and no one should approach the other. The Pequots grossly underestimated, however, the long history and experience that that British had with war, and British tensions ran high. They had reached what they considered to be a point of no return, and they were not going to let things lie. The only solution would be to end the Pequots and take that land once for all. In order to do so, they planned an attack that would stun everyone.

The English approached Mohegan and Narragansett tribes and expressed their desire to take out the Pequots. Not all the tribes were friends at the time, and the Mohegans and Narragansetts agreed on the principal that in war, it would remain a battle between men only. No women or children would be harmed. The English, perhaps knowing they were lying through their teeth, obliged to that standard and successfully equipped themselves with the assistance of their new allies and planned their deadly and sneaky approach.

On the night of May 26, 1637, Captains John Mason and John Underhill led their men and their native allies to surround the Pequot fort on the hill in Mystic. They trod forward into the deep, dark hours of the night, prepared to attack at dawn. The men found two entrances that could be utilized and immediately blockaded both. The Pequot terrain was a well-palisaded fort on a steep hill for best defensibility. One of the British soldiers described the fort as such:

> They choose a piece of ground dry and of best advantage, forty or fifty foote square. (But this was at least 2 acres of ground.) here they pitch close together, as they can young trees and halfe trees, as thicke as a mans thigh, or the calfe of his legge. Ten or twelve foote high they are above the ground, and within rammed three foote deepe, with undermining, the earth being cast up for their better shelter against the enemies dischargements. Betwixt these pallisades are divers loope-holes, through which they let flie their winged messengers. The doore for the most part is entered side-waies, which they stop with boughes or bushes as need requireth. The space within is full of Wigwams.

Dawn approached, and Mason and Underhill sent all their English soldiers, totaling fewer than 120, into the fort and left the natives outside the fort to take down any attempting escapees. As they began their attack within the fort, they entered into the wigwams, slaughtering whomever they encountered, be them men, women, children or the elderly. It was, in fact, documented that many of the men were out in the woods hunting and only one-third of the population in the fort at Mystic that night were men. Two-thirds of the slumbering populace at the time of the attack was women and children.

The Mohegans and Narragansetts were caught by nasty surprise. In the British wars that these colonial settlers had been trained in, no one was spared, regardless of age or gender. It was clear they had lied about their war tactics in order to gain alliance. Some of the native allies departed in the dark, horrified by the brutality inflicted on the women and children, while others stood there in shock, repeating the words, "It's too much. It's too much." Finally, some of the other tribal members, not knowing what else to do and not wanting to jeopardize the well-being of their own, continued to assist in battle against the Pequots.

Since the men were good warriors and their women were aptly trained as well, numerous British soldiers were injured severely and a couple even killed during the unforeseen attack. Mason and Underhill did not like the tone that this battle had taken in hand-to-hand combat and felt that the English were too susceptible to casualty. Thus, Mason promptly summoned his men outside the fort, continuing to block off any exits.

Captain Mason then famously proclaimed the murderous words, "We must burn them!" Others documented that he more cryptically proclaimed, "Let them burn!" Regardless of the words Mason chose for his fatal proclamation, he promptly ordered his men and his remaining allies to set fire to the fort and surround it in an impenetrable circle so that no one could escape. If anyone escaped, he or she would be shot dead by the British or taken down by the surrounding circle of Narragansett and Mohegan allies. It was set up so that all residents in the Pequot fort would die by fire or trying to escape.

Mason proudly recounted the evening, saying, "And indeed such a dreadful Terror did the Almighty let fall upon their Spirits, that they would fly from us and run into the very Flames, where many of them perished. And when the Fort was thoroughly Fired, Command was given, that all should fall off and surround the Fort; which was readily attended by all."

In less than one hour, all but fourteen Native Americans within that fort perished. It took not even a precious sixty minutes for hundreds upon

Nineteenth-century Pequot War engraving. *Image courtesy of Wikipedia.*

hundreds of Pequots to burn to death surrounded by inescapable flames. If at first thought the event couldn't be more tragic, the fact also remained that the majority of the deceased were women and children. Unofficial counts indicate that somewhere between four hundred and seven hundred Native Americans passed away that horrifying night. Of the fourteen documented survivors, seven were sold into slavery and seven were believed to have escaped the rings of their tormentors that surrounded their fort that evening.

John Mason declared, "And thus in little more than one Hour's space was their impregnable Fort with themselves utterly Destroyed, to the Number of six or seven Hundred, as some of themselves confessed. There were only seven taken Captive and about seven escaped."

Nearby Pequot tribes attempted to come to the Mystic River fort when they heard of the incident to provide any help and found only overwhelming death and sadness. There was nothing that could be done. Just a few short weeks later, all the Englishmen attempted to find the surviving Pequots and kill them, or if they appeared to be good, sturdy men, they sold them into slavery. John Mason stated, "About a Fortnight after our Return home, which was about one Month after the Fight at Mistick, there Arrived in Pequot

River several Vessels from the Massachusetts, Captain Isreal Stoughton being Commander in Chief; and with him about One hundred and twenty Men; being sent by that Colony to pursue the War against the Pequots."

Of the Pequot population, 1,500 were either killed in the massacre and the subsequent manhunt or sold into a lifetime of slavery. All of these tragic events were deemed the Pequot War. After a nearly two-year saga of horror and attacks came to an end, nearly eliminating all surviving Pequots in Connecticut, the Treaty of Hartford brought the war to an end in 1638.

Any trust existing between the settlers and other Native Americans was short-lived at this point as word spread of what happened. It only took forty years for the British to turn on their allies the Narragansetts, who would meet a similar fate. The attacks, in fact, continued for hundreds of years across the country on all Native American tribes.

The Mystic Massacre was the event that set the tone for what overcame the Native Americans and the nation for years after and was, in fact, the very first in a slew of such acts of brutality. This hour of time on May 26, 1637, changed the world and the pioneering days of our nation eternally. It's hard to say what could have been so many years ago, and all the what if's don't change what happened on that fateful night that the very first residents who cultivated the land of Mistick went up in flames.

Captains Mason and Underhill went to their graves believing with their whole hearts that they did the right thing and rid the world of sinners, paving the way for their colony to be formed. As so many do in religious battles or battles of land, no one believes they are in the wrong, and it all comes as a result of cultures, societies or groups of people who have lost their willingness to understand and live beside one another in a civil, thriving manner. For some time, a statue even stood in Mystic commemorating Mason himself for his successful conquest of Mystic. This monument, however, was later moved to his hometown of Windsor due to an understandable controversy raised in the community over its constant reminder of such an awful event.

Captain Mason documented his pride in his personal writings and depicted the graphic scenes, noting that you could not walk through the river community without stepping on or over the bodies of all the departed. In the same breath, he admired what a service he had done and what a triumph he had made for God, writing, "But God was above them, who laughed at his Enemies and the Enemies of his People to Scorn, making them as a fiery Oven: Thus were the Stout Hearted spoiled, having slept their last Sleep, and none of their Men could find their Hands: Thus did the Lord judge among the Heathen, filling the Place with dead Bodies!"

Commemorative statue of John Mason on Pequot Avenue, erected circa 1925. *Photo courtesy of the Mystic River Historical Society, Inc., Mystic, Connecticut.*

Mason never did remark on what was done with those bodies, and to be sure, many of them were taken in by the earth that they had cultivated so well as days, months and years elapsed. Perhaps some were put into shallow graves, providing a semblance of proper burial for what remained of their once warrior bodies.

Underhill and Mason had definitely painted a clear picture to their fellow settlers and to their English brethren at home by submitting their accounts to a newspaper and scribing accounts in their logs.

An event like this, a massacre in its truest form, inherently left an eternal imprint on the land and has come to haunt Mystic land in a very untraditional sense, always reminding those who make their home here of what became of the first cultivators and inhabitants of the land. Indeed, after much research, it would seem fair to assess that the attack that caused the Pequot community to go up in flames has cursed the surrounding area to meet devastating fire in the dead of night for all eternity. Mystic will forever be forced to rebuild after highly destructive fires.

When one thinks of curses, they often imagine someone nearing their death and seeking revenge, muttering curses upon a land, person or family right before they meet their end. With their last mutterings comes a string

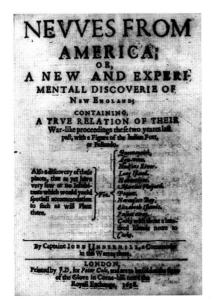

Accounts of the Pequot War as reported by Captain John Underhill in an English newspaper entitled *News from America. Photo courtesy of the Library of Congress.*

of incidents that can't help but be tied to that curse. There are examples of this from the stoning of Giles Corey in the Salem Witch Trials all the way to voodoo priestess curses in the modern-day swamps of New Orleans.

We can never know what the Native Americans who burned to death in their homes on the night of May 27 said or felt as their world crumbled around them and their lives left their bodies. Regardless of whether any curse was muttered or thought in those final moments, the event left its imprint on the land. The cries, screams, blood and tears that filled the air during that fateful evening as fire erupted through the Mystic hilltop was likely enough in and of itself to curse the developing Mystic community with a continuing series of devastating fires and a residual haunting. Rarely—if ever—do the fires that plague Mystic lead to the demise of residents and proprietors, but they always force the near complete rebuilding of the community's cultural and societal treasures.

A complete account of all the fires that have decimated Mystic landmarks could quickly become a book of its own. However, some of the more recent incidents of note from the 1800s to the 2000s successfully demonstrate the continuity and unpredictability with which these fires occur around the New London County community. Sometimes the fires come in a hastening hurricane rising up the East Coast, and other times they come without any remarkable cause of which to speak of in the quiet dead of a dark night.

One building that remains fresh in the minds of Mystic residents for its repetitive destruction by fire was most recently known as the Central Hall building. The building, once known as Floral Hall, seemed to be the fire curse's favorite place to strike for literally hundreds of years. The Central Hall once stood where part of the drawbridge and now a large fenced-off area in the downtown Mystic community can be seen. Each and every building that stood there—regardless of whether it was serving as a political pulpit for

Central Hall as it first stood in Mystic, circa 1860s. *Photo courtesy of the Mystic River Historical Society, Inc., Mystic, Connecticut.*

speakers such as Lloyd Garrison and Julia Ward House, an entertainment venue for shows, a roller-skating rink or even a more unremarkable office and business space—would come to suffer irreparable damage from nighttime fires. Floral Hall burnt down in 1863, and its successors burnt down subsequently in 1880, again in 1910 and, most recently, in 2000. By 1910, the Central Hall had stood as the oldest and largest building on West Main Street and was already suffering its third catastrophic sequence of flames. Newspaper accounts indicate that the fire was so large that neighboring towns had to send their fire crews in to assist.

By the turn of the twentieth century, Mystic residents and reporters had already begun to notice a pattern, and with the 1910 burning of the Central Hall, the hunt was on for the Mystic firebug. Regarding that very incident, the New London–area newspaper the *Day* reported on the fiery events with the headline "Mystic's Firebug Causes Damage of $40,000 Today: Morgan Block Containing Theatre, Masonic Hall, and Several Stores Destroyed Early This Morning—Grain Elevator Near Depot Burns at Same Time, There Being No Fire Apparatus to Spare from Bigger Blaze." Residents simply could not determine the cause of this event, nor the ones prior to it. Was there an arsonist? Were there early electrical failures? Was Mother Nature taking Mystic in her fury? The first guesses and results of preliminary investigation suggested arson. The *Day*'s report provided some details:

Mystic people have become finally aroused to a sense of the situation and it is probable that as a result of this last blaze efforts will be made to locate the firebug. Some of the businessmen here who have gotten tired of waiting for the authorities to act have engaged watchmen to look after their property during the night. Everyone seems to feel satisfied now that a firebug is at work in the village, and that the only way to get rid of the probability of more fires at any time is to find the firebug. An insurance detective has been at work in the village for the last two weeks, but he has met with no success as yet and so far as is known no one seems to be under suspicion. Unless the incendiary work is stopped very soon it will mean increased fire insurance rates in Mystic, and it is up to the merchants here to do something on their own account.

Less than one hundred years later, long after rebuilding from the 1910 fire, Central Hall met its fourth and final set of blazes. As the twenty-first century rapidly approached, Mystic decided to remorsefully acknowledge the loss of its largest and most lively downtown building and bid it a final goodbye. A total of eight businesses were lost in 2000. After so much effort and so much money for its repeated resurrections, Mystic simply could not take another chance. Thus, the downtown landscape possesses a vacant hole where the building once stood, and it is marked only by a wooden fence.

In between all the burnings of the Central Hall building, other downtown establishments found that they were no strangers to the raging blazes, either. A large meetinghouse once stood in Mystic at the corner of East Main and Cottrell Street. In 1885, a fire ravaged the building almost completely, but the community came together and resurrected its unique piece of history, transforming it into an opera house. Unfortunately, it only took fifteen years for blazes to wreak havoc on the premises once again. The local *Mystic Journal* reported in 1900, "All that remains are sides up to the second story window including the charred remains of the interior." It took the community some more time to gather themselves and their purse strings before coming to rebuild again, but sure enough, the land was prime real estate, and the Mystic community missed the theatrical presence that the opera house had come to provide. The Strand Theatre opened as the new local cinema, with an accompanying storefront on the land where the opera house once stood. Construction was completed in the 1920s, and the businesses thrived. Another dry goods shop even opened up there in the 1950s. Thinking that the fiery episodes were finally behind them and that maybe they had been due to the wooden structures and old wiring, Mystic's new riverfront block appeared safe from harm. Unfortunately, relief would be short-lived, as a raging fire came at the crack of dawn one morning to decimate that entire area of landscape once more to a degree of epic proportions.

The fire that stole the newly opened movie theater and all kinds of neighboring businesses is still discussed and known throughout the region. It was officially deemed the "Mystic Fire of 1960." Residents claim that they awoke from their beds at just about dawn (paralleling the timing of the massacre), astonished by the sight of the sky enveloped in smoke. Some first thought that perhaps the town was under attack. The smoke blocked out the sunrise, frightening the entire populace. In the east side of downtown Mystic, on what was then called Newbury Block, the fire annihilated nine stores, the theater and six offices. Just over one hundred years earlier, in 1858, the very same geographic location was taken by a blaze that claimed a hotel that once sat by the water. Much like what happened during the conflagration that took Central Hall in 1910, multiple companies were called from the neighboring communities to put out the blazes. When all was said and done on December 12, 1960, a hardware company, a window company, a laundromat, a plumber's office, a pharmacy, a barbershop, a newsstand and more had been lost. The entire downtown landscape was repainted and would never be the same again.

The 1900s was a time of great growth in the community, and perhaps that's why the fires came with such a seeming vengeance. To be sure, not one inch of the downtown landscape would be unscathed, be it on the Groton side or the Stonington side. The fiery curse had no bounds. Just after the Opera House burning of 1900 and the Central Hall's third burning in 1910 came the Gilbert Block fire of 1915. The Gilbert Block had only been built in 1909 and was proudly hailed as the new business center of Mystic. It cost $80,000 when it was constructed, quite a pretty penny during those times. One morning, just as dawn approached, a fire took the building, with damages estimated at $75,000, almost the entire cost of the original building. The *Mystic Journal* reported that the fire started on the uppermost floor in a theater. With the water having been shut down for the night, the local firemen encountered a lack of adequate water pressure, and the fire progressed too quickly to be controlled. Neighboring fire companies returned to Mystic once more and prevented the flames from spreading beyond the Gilbert Block.

Another cursed block didn't have much time to pick up the pieces after a 1960 fire. On West Main Street in downtown Mystic is an area known as the Avery Block. The Avery Block had been there for nearly two hundred years.

In the mid-1800s, the block housed a furniture store and coffin and mortuary services. It was set up to be a two-business establishment. For undocumented reasons, the building with the mortuary was later sold, and in 1880, a man named F.B Smith sold plumbing supplies and furnaces next door to the still thriving furniture shop. Some claim that a fire occurred in what was once the mortuary half in the mid-1800s, and in the 1880s, something else happened to the building. It was again undocumented but rumored to be a fire that requiring rebuilding. This was followed by about eighty safe years until a fire took the block in 1975. In 1975, the *Day* wrote yet again about the repetition of neighborhood fires with the headline "Mystic Fire One of Many." The article went on to say, "The East Main Street and Cottrell Street area that was hit by fire early this morning has a history of serious fires."

Not giving up hope on the dear old Avery Block, residents rebuilt once more, and it stands to this day, harboring new and thriving local businesses.

The 1975 fire did not just take the Avery Block in its wake. It also took the majority of the still standing Whaler's Inn. Whaler's Inn sits on the corner of East Main and Cottrell Streets. The Whaler's Inn has gone by varying names over the years as a landmark local establishment.

The inn had just skated by, surviving the 1960 fire, when new owners came into the establishment in 1965 to do extensive renovations and reopen the doors for a brand-new start. In 1975, the fire destroyed the building,

Corner of East Main and Cottrell Streets, the site of the Whaler's Inn, circa 1925. *Photo courtesy of the Mystic River Historical Society, Inc., Mystic, Connecticut.*

including some structural elements over one hundred years old. It was said that nothing at all could be salvaged. Based on the designs and remaining structure, Whaler's Inn's owners picked themselves up by the bootstraps and restored the entire establishment, which still stands as a beautiful landmark to view in downtown Mystic.

In 1874, the Mystic Fire Department's Hoxie Firehouse once sat on Holmes Street, not far from some of our other local haunts, but in 1897, the building went up in flames, prompting the fire department to establish its new building on nearby Cottrell Street. This building also burned down about forty years later, sometime in the 1940s. Again, perhaps the third time was the charm, so the Hoxie Firehouse was brought back to life on its new location on Broadway in 1992, where it still sits, fire free to this day. Similarly, the Hook and Ladder Firehouse, built in 1884 on the now historic district of Gravel Street, didn't even last thirty years when blazes took the structure in 1912. The firemen repaired the structure, expanding to fit a ladder truck. However, it was ultimately decided to move the headquarters of the Mystic Fire Department in the 1960s, leaving the Gravel Street firehouse behind.

Corner of East Main and Cottrell Streets, circa 2014. *Photo by Shelby McInvale.*

Hoxie Firehouse on Cottrell Street, circa 1925. *Photo from the Dickinson Collection, courtesy of the Mystic River Historical Society, Inc., Mystic, Connecticut.*

The original devastation of fire which took the Pequot community from Mystic and upon which colonists cultivated and created their settlement set the tone for a community to be plagued by an otherwise inexplicable propensity for fires. The fort was a home, a resting place and a gathering place, a true village-like community in which the Pequot Indians lived, worked and thrived. In a sense, the last Pequot fort was the first downtown of Mystic. The current downtown landscape where the locals shop, meet and work is presently the prime setting for such targeted blazes. As evidenced by all the newspaper articles, the most ravaging and mysterious fires come in the early morning hours just around dawn, the same time that the Pequot fort went up in blazes. Never has blame been placed on a suspect and never have building occupants or tenants suffered ill harm, but the community members are always forced to open their wallets, pour out money and rebuild—only to have their local landmarks and institutions taken away by flames again. Mystic developed into a community founded on the fiery demise of others, destined to rebuild and conquer fire after fire throughout the landscape.

It is commonly believed that when spirits pass so quickly with no expectation or if they pass in a violent manner, their souls become stuck between here and the afterlife, trying to make sense of what happened and come to terms with their own death. Could it be that the hundreds of souls of the original fire victims are still stuck somewhere in a limbo, reliving their fiery horror? An eternity of enduring that kind of event would seem excessively cruel, and likely there are spirits that are reliving that treacherous and deadly night. The spirits look over Mystic with wary eyes to be sure that the structures their residents covet or take pride in too deeply are taken in the night without warning or hesitation. The fiery curse serves as a constant reminder of how quickly something of value can be taken from us.

Chapter 2

THE PROTECTIVE CAPTAIN
AND THE PLAYFUL NIECE

CAPTAIN DANIEL PACKER INNE
RESTAURANT AND PUB

If you head down Water Street in Mystic as night slowly approaches you will find yourself at a landmark dating back hundreds of years. Looking at the building, you may find your eyes averted to the top floor window, feeling as if you're being watched. However, you'll quickly be distracted by the grandeur of the colonial architecture before you. The striking former inn is the Captain Daniel Packer Inne Restaurant and Pub.

Approaching the historic establishment, visitors find themselves filled with excitement and wonder, knowing that each and every time they get closer, they will have some sort of spine-tingling sensation. In a local ghost tour, I spin the restaurant's legendary tales to tour guests. Tales are of the formidable captain and his playful great-grandniece from the decades of yore who continue to frequent, reside in or visit the old inn, despite their departure from this world so many decades ago. Without fail, there is the continual eerie and sometimes accurate consciousness that they ever so knowingly peer out those windows at passersby. Occasionally, outside the Captain Daniel Packer Inne, tourists seeking local haunted spots get an incredible stroke of luck and receive first-hand accounts from staff members of the ghostly encounters that go on within the restaurant walls.

What I am beginning to call the Daniel Packer experience is ever evolving, and having become the "ghost lady" of Mystic, I often am approached on the street by locals with stories of their own ghostly sightings. Admittedly, a great number of these took place at the Captain Daniel Packer Inne. Whether the local is a long-lost family descendant of the Captain, a former

View of Water Street, circa 1925. *Photo from the Dickinson Collection, courtesy of the Mystic River Historical Society, Inc., Mystic, Connecticut.*

employee or just a frequent guest of the inn, the spirits view all visits as prime opportunities to imprint and make themselves known (sometimes in the form of a full apparition). What makes the tales so particularly haunting (pun intended) is the fact that all the sightings can be narrowed down to specific ghosts that are known by name.

The Captain Daniel Packer Inne has been a landmark property, inn and restaurant in Mystic since its erection in 1754. The main part of the house was solidly constructed, and a porch and other expansions were added in the early 1800s. The current restaurant and former inn sits just toward the end of Water Street.

The building was constructed by its namesake, Captain Daniel Packer, who earned his rank of captain in the Revolutionary War, where he was responsible for delivering arms and goods to the army. Though named a captain at war, Mr. Packer was also a captain of the sea, known as a famous square-rigger in the rapidly developing New England landscape. Generation after generation in the Packer family would continue the legacy of becoming seafaring men, all earning the title of captain. It is well documented that the Packer men utilized the secure and helpful placement of their homestead and inn to bravely assist in defending British attacks on Mystic during the War of 1812. Rest assured the Packer women would do their part as well. In fact, Daniel's daughter Sabrina and her husband, Eldridge, were credited with building the *Polly*, the first recorded ship put into the Mystic River.

Tracking backward to the mid-1700s to our original captain and founder of the inn, it should be noted that Daniel Packer had a very definitive and significant role in the seafaring nature of the riverfront locale where he resided. Captain Packer owned and operated a venture known as Packer Landing, a rope ferry that carried guests and travelers across the Mystic River. The travel stop on Water Street, which served as the initial takeoff point for the ferry, was an inn at the time. Travelers going between New York and Boston, equipped with horses and stagecoaches, could spend the night and enjoy a superb meal while waiting to cross the river via ferry. Daniel Packer loved having guests and family over to his establishment and enjoyed even more thoroughly being able to take guests across the river, telling tales of the war and of his days at sea. He was a chatty man and full of pride, a well-loved local in Mystic.

Some of his guests may have included former president George Washington, who, it is rumored, he knew during the Revolutionary War and who was known to travel through Mystic in the 1700s. The captain never did journal on that definitively, but he did make sure to document that he invited members of a traveling circus to stay in his inn and that they, in fact, did. This, in turn, allowed him to tell all the ferry guests that lions, monkeys and all sorts of imaginable creatures spent a night in his very own home.

The captain and his wife, Hanna, raised seven children in their home. As one may imagine, the place was always bustling with activity and excitement, including lots of visits from family members, who loved to spend all their time at the inn enjoying the grandeur and time with their relatives and guests. The captain remained the inn's proprietor until the end of his days and vowed to always take care of and watch over his inn. Many would say he still is protecting the inn and visiting with the new guests, almost as if he never left.

When Daniel's children had grown and passed on the inn to their children, life on Water Street continued to thrive. Many, many Packer family descendants would eventually manage the family property. The children continued to have children of their own, all the while passing down the tradition of operating the family inn (which also sometimes served as a residence).

One of these descendants, Captain Daniel's great-grandson Captain Charles Carroll Packer, was born in the homestead in 1833. When not at sea, he resided with his wife, Fannie Morse (of the Morse family who founded the Reliance Machine Company at Factory Square up the road), and his children. Since the house had continued to serve as a safe and entertaining

The Captain Daniel Packer Inne, circa 1925. *Photo from the Dickinson Collection, courtesy of the Mystic River Historical Society, Inc., Mystic, Connecticut*

place for extended family to visit, it sometimes became a second home for a loved one in need. This happened in the 1800s when Captain Charles Carroll's sister-in-law "Muddie" Morse Clift resided there after the passing away of her husband, Lieutenant Amos Clift. The pain of being alone in the Clift family home on Gravel Street was too much to bear after his death, so Mrs. Clift and her daughter Ada, Charles's niece, moved into the spacious homestead. Ada was said to have loved being at the Packer family home more than anything. Unfortunately, at the young age of seven years and eight months, Ada Byron Clift's time at the Water Street home was cut drastically short. Having been plagued with scarlet fever, little Ada passed away quietly in her sleep one evening. The year was 1874. Though Ada may have left the family property physically, it seems that she did not let death end her time at the house. Instead, Ada thought it may be a good place to spend some of her eternity.

Unfortunately, as decades pass, the economy, weather and the like can take a toll on a family and a property, and by the 1970s, the Captain Daniel Packer Inne had seen some better days. The home had gotten pretty run down, and in Mystic, there was a lot of controversy over what to do with the property, whether to keep it or wait for a brave soul to renovate it. Some suggested that it be torn down and condominiums be built. Finally, the answer

This 1910 postcard depicts Mystic's Gravel Street. *Image courtesy of the Mystic River Historical Society, Inc., Mystic, Connecticut.*

came. A couple named Richard and Lulu Kiley decided they saw a diamond in the rough and took over the property in 1979. They were the first family not descended from Captain Daniel Packer to take over the home, but they put their heart and soul into it, pouring out all of their energy to make it a flourishing property once again. Renovations took four years and included preservation of the original fireplaces, mantles and beams dating back to the 1700s. The Kileys successfully turned the inn into a highly acclaimed restaurant in Connecticut that is now frequented by visitors from around the world. The captain himself could not have been more pleased.

When visiting Mystic, you must be sure to add having a meal at the Captain Daniel Packer Inne to your agenda. The cuisine could be described as both delicious and exquisite. The renovated inn has an authentic colonial ambience, an indescribable view and drinks that could warm the coldest soul on a winter's evening. Should you find yourself dining here in the fall and winter months, the inn serves up a concoction of apple cider and local cinnamon apple–infused moonshine. It is pure delight.

It seems fitting that a place so rich with history, tradition, family and local importance be home to some of the most popular and well-acquainted ghosts in Mystic. As you may surmise, the frequently sighted spirits include Captain Daniel Packer himself and, perhaps even more frequently, the young Ada Clift.

Dating back to the purchase of the property in 1979, unexplained paranormal tales from the Packer descendants had already been conveyed to the new purchasers. On top of this, the Kileys received a visit from an elderly woman claiming that she herself was a direct descendant of Captain Daniel Packer. She looked at the new entrepreneurs and at the building as she explained that she was visiting because the captain appeared to her in a dream and told her that he was unhappy with what was becoming of his property. The new owners told the woman that when they were through with renovations, she and the captain would be quite pleased with the finished product, as they were going to restore the property to its original glory. The woman begged to disagree and made her exit. Naturally, the Kileys assumed that the elderly woman had heard rumors that the building would be torn down and must have still been concerned.

As the months passed into years and the renovations were done, the changes to the building—which had served as a homestead, an inn and finally a restaurant—were miraculous. The elderly woman showed up at 32 Water Street once more asking to speak to the new owners. They were glad to see her again, hoping she'd be pleased. She looked around once more and then peered back at them and said, "You will not be seeing me again. The captain came to me in my dreams once more last night and said he is quite pleased with what you've done with the place. It looks perfect, and he will be looking in on it." Sure, it all sounded a bit strange, but it was kind of a nice relief to think the original builder and—at the very least—his descendant thought they had done the family property more than its justice. The elderly woman was correct, too, for they never did see her again. The captain, however, was another matter.

When Mr. Kiley was in the midst of the renovations, he continued to meet with the previous owners and conveyed to them some of his strange experiences. One thing he noted was that a lot of the workers and staff members at the time reported seeing a sea captain at various places only to have him disappear upon approach. As renovations neared a finish, the captain was seen a bit less but never stopped making his appearances. Some staff members continue to report sighting a vanishing sea captain to this day. Could this possibly be the original Captain Daniel? Others, including descendants of the Packer family, think it's perhaps Captain Charles Carroll Packer. The owner prior to the Kileys, Mr. Charles Carroll Keeler, believed it was indeed his namesake and made claim in his personal documents that growing up he was told that Grandfather Packer, who passed away in the 1800s, still lived there, and all strange noises were generally attributed to him.

Whichever captain it may be—perhaps both—he does, in fact, look in and protect the place, particularly from the fires that the Mystic area is so cursed by. On not one but two occasions, an unforeseen force led to the disruption of a potential major fire in the making. One evening, a night manager called Mr. Kiley and spoke of smelling smoke in the bar area. When the owner arrived, he found a frayed wire laying on the stone foundation emitting a very small amount of smoke. Thinking this was it, he ventured to the electrical panel and turned off the corresponding appliance attached to that particular wire and departed in the wee hours of the morning. Just a short time later, the night manager, who was trying to depart, felt stopped by an unseen force. She tried to exit the door and simply could not. The manager simply was not being allowed to leave. In a frenzied panic from such a strange sensation, the manager called the owner, and he arrived at the restaurant once more. Upon Mr. Kiley's arrival, he and the manager went down to the bar area, where the smell of smoke was even stronger. It turns out that the wrong appliance had been turned off, and the wire had turned red hot. If left all night, a major fire would have been certain. When the correct appliance was unplugged, the unseen force let both individuals depart without hesitation.

Fire tried once more to claim the Captain Daniel Packer Inne in a similarly sneaky way. A bartender closing up from a shift alone was used to his routine. There were two doors to lock up at night. One he locked from the inside, and the other he locked from the outside upon exit. Every single night, he locked the innermost door and walked outside the door facing Water Street. One evening, as he was preparing to go about his usual

Sign outside the present-day Captain Daniel Packer Inne Restaurant and Pub.

routine, he felt an unseen force stop him from going out his usual exit and prompt him to go to the other exit. Thinking it odd, he figured it was best to appease this unseen force—or, at the very least, his conscience—and he departed through the other door. Once he departed, he noted a large fire had already started in the dumpster outside. He was able to call the fire department and have the fire extinguished. If he had not seen it when he did, it was believed the fire could have taken down the whole restaurant.

Due to the protective nature of the captains and their duty to protect the homestead and inn, Mystic locals have always assumed it was Daniel or perhaps even Charles Packer who protected their establishment from the curse of Mystic fires.

Captains must have their fun also. It was rumored that Captain Daniel Packer was quite the prankster and perhaps plays pranks to this day. Rather than his apparition being sighted often throughout the property, he has more compelling jokes to play. There was a mysterious instance of a soaring glass in the bar that almost seemed to have been thrown in an act of excited jest. One evening in the crowded bar, all the tables and stools were filled. The glass rack above the bartenders' heads seemed as it always did, nothing to remark about. Without warning, one of the glasses flew off the rack, out from under the bar area, across three tables of dining patrons and smashed against the stone wall. The witnesses were numerous employees and guests alike. When the glass shattered, the entire room stared in amazement. What? Who? How did this happen? The answer simply never came. Since the only other ghost is that of a small girl, this led the staff to believe that it was one of the captain's pranks maybe gone a little too far.

Other antics attributed to the captain or captains include the slamming of the bar door during cleaning or quiet times, the stomping of boots and the starting of fires in the fireplace on a cold winter's day. For the most part, the previous owner and founder seems to be looking out for the place or is simply enjoying another walk around or time with his guests. Perhaps he's checking in on dear Ada. She, of course, seems to appear even more often than the Captain himself.

I had heard countless rumors of the haunts at Captain Daniel Packer Inne, and so I set up a meeting with Allie, the daughter of the Kiley family who purchased the property in 1979 and who serves currently as the general manager. It would seem that the spirits were quite cognizant of our upcoming meeting. At the original scheduled time of our meeting, Allie had fallen ill and had to cancel. Her staff kindly directed me to call in a few days when she might be feeling better and returned to work in order to set our inevitable rain date. A few days passed, and I was caught up with some family business before I was able to call. I tried to get through a few times, and the line kept saying that my call could not be placed at this time and to please try again later. Other times it would ring into silence and nothing would happen, almost with a strange echo. Finally, I grabbed the phone and dialed the number one more time—no auto save, no redial; just hitting the numbers—and the call still could not be placed. What the heck, I thought? This is the restaurant number. The mobile phone finally placed the call, and Allie picked it up. We decided to meet the next day. When I arrived and met Allie, she remarked to me, "It was the strangest thing when you called. I had just picked up the post-it with your name on it and said, 'Oh, hopefully she'll call soon' and went to throw it in the trash when the phone rang and it was you." I exchanged my story about the phone's antics, and we laughed, wondering what the spirits were getting at.

Allie began to tell me some tales of the inn's history, and when she was talking as we stood in the banquet hall on the third floor of the restaurant, I thought I saw a young person run behind her, giggle and then run off into the kitchen. I thought nothing of it. It was just us upstairs and perhaps another staff member in the office in back. I thought one of them may have had their daughter with her. The odd thing was that my husband who was there and Allie didn't seem to acknowledge her, and I never saw her again. As Allie began to tell me about a little spirit named Ada, I heard the giggle but saw no one. Chills ran up my spine. Was I experiencing her already? Was it this easy? I made sure to look as though nothing was happening. I didn't want to appear crazy. I was already there looking for good ghost stories! I now am confident that it was Ada I heard and she was simply quite pleased to hear stories of her antics being relayed with a warm heart. Ada has indeed been the subject of so many stories, and what follows are just a mere few that do her the most justice.

It was a brisk February a couple of years back, and Valentine's Day was approaching quickly. For a fine dining restaurant, it is a holiday of preparation and importance. When Allie was preparing for the holiday by setting up the décor of the restaurant, she realized that she had a great deal of pink, red and white balloons to blow up. Not wanting to tackle the daunting task alone, she called her good friend to come over and assist. Her good friend had a young daughter about eight years old at the time who she brought with her. While the manager and her friend blew up the balloons, the young girl seemed to be enjoying herself, playing around the restaurant, laughing and giggling. Not wanting to interrupt her to inquire, the friends assumed that she was playing with an imaginary friend and had a great imagination. After a short while, the girl approached her mom and explained with frustration, "I've been playing hide-and-seek with this little girl who keeps calling my name. I can hear, but I just can't see her or find her anywhere. She says her name is Ada." The manager and her friend exchanged a quick glance knowingly.

Captain Daniel Packer Inne Restaurant and Pub, circa 2014.

The young girl knew nothing of the Ada from years past at the inn, so they brushed it off and told her perhaps she could play with her another time. On rare occasions, the girl still wonders when her mom visits the restaurant if Ada is there to play with her, and they inform her that Ada is not there that day. Children are often highly sensitive to the presence of spirits. With their innocence and lack of judgment, spirits can often feel welcome in the world of a child, almost as if to live again.

Unfortunately, adults aren't always as welcome to our ghostly friends as children seem to be. However, this does not mean that the livelier spirits don't make themselves known to the "grown-ups" of the world and seek out those who are perhaps (sometimes unknowingly) more sensitive than others. Ada has proven to be one of those lively spirits. The restaurant layout contains the pub on the ground level, fine dining on the first level and a second level for buffets or professional reservation dinners—private parties, if you will. A door on the first floor leads up to the second floor via a staircase that fits the colonial feel of the house. The staircase up to the second floor is one of the two places where Ada likes to be seen the most.

One evening, a couple had made reservations on the first floor to enjoy an elegant and luxurious anniversary dinner. Upon arrival, the hostess kindly escorted them to the table located in view of the doorway opening to the staircase for the second floor. The gentleman inquired of the hostess, "What's behind that door?"

"Oh, that leads to our banquet hall upstairs for private parties," she replied. The gentleman repeated himself, "No, what's behind that door?" Perhaps he was looking for a more detailed response. The hostess responded once more, "It's our banquet hall upstairs for private parties, but it's empty right now. I promise you won't be disturbed."

Getting irritated, the man asked once more, "What's behind that door right now?" The hostess thought for a second, truly wondering what he could be referring to. Before she had time to respond, the man interrupted, "There is a little girl behind that door, and she is dead. Why would you keep a little girl behind the door?" He became quite irate, took his wife by the arm and proclaimed, "We are leaving."

Another occurrence happened in that very same vicinity—in fact, in the stairwell. Two women who were invited to dine on the second floor for a private party made their way up the stairs and, upon arrival, seemed quite perturbed. When they met with the waitstaff, they said, "You know, it's very rude to let a little girl be standing in the middle of the stairwell bouncing a ball while people are trying to walk by. She doesn't even move!" The waitstaff looked quite confused, as did the other guests at the party. Neither they nor anyone else saw any young girl in the stairway playing ball. There had been no children in the stairwell or in the restaurant all day. The two women, however, were certain the little girl was there, clear as day.

Those women were not the only guests who assumed they saw a child who was very much alive. In fact, that is a common statement when a guest has an Ada sighting. One evening, an elderly woman was enjoying a meal with her family when she excused herself to the ladies' room. Moments later when she departed the ladies' room, the older woman looked very bothered and grabbed the nearest staff member, demanding to speak to a manager. The manager approached the woman, asking her what was wrong. The woman responded, "You really shouldn't allow little girls to run around the bathroom unsupervised, just giggling and running. She almost tripped me. It's very rude." The staff looked around the restroom and around the restaurant, finding not one small child or young girl who could have been the culprit.

Perhaps it's a good laugh for young Ada to catch people quite indisposed. A younger local Mystic man whose dad used to be a chef in the restaurant and had experiences with Ada or strange sensations that she was there just running around and giggling also had a tale to tell. The young man detailed that he himself was there one evening enjoying the night with friends and had to use the restroom. As he washed his hands and looked up in the mirror, he saw directly behind him a young girl standing there giggling and then running off. He said he didn't say a word as the hairs on his arm stood on end. He simply knew it was her, and he was no stranger to the stories of how she loved to spy on people in bathrooms. He was just the most recent on a long list of those with restroom sightings of Ada.

Oftentimes when a guest's first encounter with Ada is upon arrival, they think she is the child of a staff member. The waitstaff indicated that at different times, either they or the hostess have received comments on their beautiful and happy daughter right behind them looking so helpful. I can only imagine the chills that shoot up their spines upon hearing such a compliment.

It would seem that if you are to visit the Captain Daniel Packer Inne in search of Ada, the stairwell and the restrooms are your best bet. There are, on occasions, other places that she makes an appearance. In fact, if we were to tally them, the third most common location of Ada sightings would be near the fireplace. One chef remarked that one day when doing some paperwork alone, he looked up when he heard a tapping and immediately noticed that the tapping came from the movement of the fireplace tools lifting up and down as if they were being played with. Ada, he wondered? The captain? He didn't stay much longer to find out and decided to finish his work another day.

One customer on the first floor was waiting at the front of the restaurant for her name to be called. The restaurant was bustling, and there was a short wait for tables. As she was glancing around, something caught her eye behind the hostess. A young girl clad in a colonial blue dress with beautiful brown hair and brown eyes was giggling away. "Watch your step," the woman called to the hostess. "There's a young girl behind you!" The customer then reported that the girl ran off to the fireplace, where she played for a moment and then disappeared. The woman had noted her period dress and found it odd, but when the young girl vanished before her eyes, she was certain she had seen a ghost. The hostess had seen no one. Unlike some other disenchanted guests, the woman thought it was a most fascinating experience and chose to finish her dining experience there.

Stories of Ada seem endless, and sometimes guests come in just looking for a glimpse of the infamous young girl. One such guest was a man whose family tree links directly back to the Packer family. He had heard so many tales that he simply had to see for himself if they were true. One evening, he called his friend and said, "I'm going to the Packer Inn for dinner, and I'm going to see Ada!" His friend wished him luck, and off he went to dine. The distant family member stayed at the restaurant for hours, enjoying his meal and whispering out loud his request for Ada to make herself known. After hours and a couple approaches to the fireplace, he was feeling a bit defeated and let down that Ada had not appeared. The gentleman went home and called his friend to report the upsetting news.

"Well, better luck next time! These things are unpredictable," his friend replied encouragingly. That night, in the middle of his sleep, the gentleman awoke to a tugging on his foot and a young child standing by his bed. He guessed that she appeared about eight years old, with brown hair and dark eyes and wearing a beautiful dress. She giggled and ran off. Wondering if his eyes deceived him, he went back to sleep and decided not to mention the issue. He had been thinking about Ada all evening. Perhaps his mind was playing tricks. The next morning, when the family descendant awoke and prepared his ritual morning coffee, his good friend telephoned him and said, "Ada came to you last night, didn't she?"

"How do you know?" he quickly replied.

The friend responded, "Well, she came to me also and wanted me to assure you it was her whom you saw."

The family descendant tells others to heed his warning that if you go out seeking Ada, be sure to pay her compliments. She's a mischievous little girl and may follow you home to play some tricks, but she can be appeased with compliments.

Tales continue to grow and resurface. In the more recent past, employees have claimed that Ada has favorite Christmas songs she plays on the radio in the quiet of the restaurant all times of year. There is also an assertion that during the renovations in the 1970s, a footprint of a young girl appeared on the floor totally alone and leading to nowhere. Other stories tell of a young girl who loves to watch the activity on Water Street and the boats on the river and who peers out the top-floor window watching the world go by. Occasionally, when strolling by for a tour, I'm certain I see a little face peering out at us from the shadows on the top floor.

The lore of the Captain Daniel Packer Inne proves to be some of the most captivating in all of Mystic, and the building is a treasure of fine dining, exquisite ambience and sprightly spirits. The locals and staff alike have all come to accept and rather pride themselves on their otherworldly visitors.

Before closing up for the night, Allie looks around and bids adieu to everyone, including the inn's more ghostly guests. Allie's father, Richard Kiley, has since passed on as well, and when saying good night in her heart to him as she looks over the establishment he so valiantly saved, she also whispers, "Goodnight, Ada, and Goodnight, Captain. I will see you tomorrow." Ada and Captain Packer may not always be visible, but Allie knows—as do all who visit and work at the Captain Daniel Packer Inne—that the former prestigious residents are always there, enjoying their visits with all the guests who continue to frequent their family inn. Daniel Packer's legacy of storytelling will surely persevere for decades to come.

Chapter 3

HOMESTEAD OF THE ELITE, SAFE HOUSE FOR THE ENSLAVED

WHITEHALL MANSION INN

America is young in developed history, especially in comparison to some of our neighbors across the pond whose history of civilization dates further back than you or I can imagine. However, the United States and, in particular, New England boast plenty of properties that have stood a true test of time spanning over centuries. These homes, establishments or structures offer us a compelling sense of what the early times of our nation would have been like. From the times of our founding fathers, these buildings housed people who lived or fought through a Civil War or a World War. Perhaps they were there at a more indigenous time in the country's past and labored over the land cultivating for growth—something hard for us to imagine as we drive to the nearest grocery store. Properties that stand through these triumphs and trials and the people who saw them through always create the perfect ambience and home for our spiritual friends who may appear in various period dress.

New England harbors many such buildings that cause us to pause for much-needed historical reflection. Mystic is no stranger to this and provides such a significant pocket of history, with explorers and residents from Europe landing in Mystic's waters long before an official founding of the country.

One property that dates back to the 1650s lies right in what may seem to be an otherwise very commercial area of Mystic, and that is the Whitehall Mansion. The building has changed almost as much as the land has been divided and repurposed over the years, but the property of the Whitehall Mansion still remains as a beautiful historic testimony where visitors and guests are still lucky enough to spend a night, as it has been converted into an inn.

The property itself—before it housed the mansion, homestead or farm—was purchased by the Gallup family, a well-known name in the Mystic community. After elder family member John Gallup passed away in 1650, after twenty years as a New England colonist, his son Captain John Gallup and his wife, Hannah, came to the Mystic area, where they applied for a land grant. Hartford colonial founders were giving out grants of land as an act of thanks for work and productive assistance. Unfortunately, the property of note was to be split, and the Gallups were granted land just a bit south of what we could call the Whitehall Farm. The Gallup family still had many surrounding areas throughout New London, but the land divisions began as more people came to Mystic, and a new minister in town named Richard Blinman was awarded 260 acres of land neighboring the Mystic River. This parcel was close to the Gallups and was the original plot where the Whitehall Mansion would be erected. Can you imagine being awarded such acreage these days in such a beautiful landscape? One would be aghast at the very thought! John Gallup sold some of the land he was awarded farther south and moved to the Mystic east bank in 1863, even closer to Whitehall, where he would build a home. The home stood close to the Elm Grove Cemetery and is no longer there, but he was able to raise his seven children there right on the heels of the Whitehall property.

Throughout the east bank of the river, grants continued to be handed out. One of these grant awardees, Robert Park, built the second home in the area, and finally the Reverend Blinman sold his grant to a Thomas Park for a brief flicker in time before it was promptly sold once more to the neighboring Gallups, bringing everything full circle in a sense. It was indeed one of John Gallup's sons, William, who constructed the first Whitehall Mansion on this new grant. It was the third house in the Whitehall area and the house that could be considered the original on the property. That particular home may not have stuck around for over 350 years, but it was that home's foundation that actually became the very foundation on which Whitehall Mansion was erected by the Woodbridge family years later and which remains to this day.

William Gallup and his wife, Sarah, had six children born between 1688 and 1701 who were raised in the home. William was an important part of local history, a member of legislature and almost a confidant and guard for the remaining Native Americans in the local area. Some of the Pequots and Mohawks actually attended the wedding of his eldest daughter, Mary, on the property. All of the Gallup daughters, in fact, wed on the family estate.

When reflecting on all these events, it's important to consider the imprint that must have been made on the land throughout all this activity and what interesting spirits who once lived through such events could be coming back to their old stomping grounds. Perhaps some visitors are there to relive that uncommon wedding ceremony, where the guest list united Native Americans and settlers alike.

In the eighteenth century, Lieutenant Gallup and his wife passed away. His children had taken different life courses and were scattered around the country. Sadly, one of his sons had died as well. The property passed down to his youngest daughter, Temperance, in the late 1720s. She held on to the property for nearly the entire remainder of her life before she gave the deeds to a man named Colonel John Williams in 1760. A mere four years later, Williams sold one hundred acres of the property to Dr. Dudley Woodbridge, who had been acquiring numerous properties in the Mystic River vicinity.

Mr. Woodbridge came from a long line of ministers in Connecticut and, in fact, studied ministry at the esteemed Yale University, from which he graduated in 1724, and he practiced in Groton for years later. In 1739, Mr. Woodbridge wed and seemingly gave up his ministerial profession to become a doctor. Where he learned his practice remains unknown, but a doctor he became before his acquisition of the Whitehall property in 1764. Woodbridge also assisted locally in the Revolutionary War. He was named to a Committee of Correspondence chartered to sympathize with the Patriots in Boston. His work continued on various committees throughout the era, culminating in his purchase of a vessel named the *Black Princess*, which boasted twelve guns and twelve men under another famous Mystic man (and Mystic ghost), Master Captain Crary.

The Woodbridge Mansion was constructed by Woodbridge's employed carpenters shortly after his purchase of the land. Records indicate that the house was completed around 1771 to 1775. His family moved in immediately. As aforementioned, the new home was built on the foundation from the Gallup home, which had fallen into disrepair and was almost completely torn down. There were rumors in town that the Woodbridge family had kept one room to almost its complete original standing and rebuilt around it. Perhaps that remains the most haunted room. The part that many believe remained during the rebuilding of the home on the foundation was on the ground floor. Interestingly enough, there was even talk among town historians that a separately hinged upper and lower door by the ground level on the south side of the basement once served as a store or, even more exciting, a local tavern in the community during the Gallup era.

The then new Woodbridge house appeared as what we may view to be a normal-sized or just somewhat larger colonial home. During the Revolutionary War era, however, it was considered to be a place of grandeur, and thus it was aptly named a mansion. The original property spanned much larger than we can imagine today, as population was low and farm area was great. The Whitehall Mansion was built close to the river atop a hill. It has moved at least two—possibly three—times over the years to protect it from the inevitable destruction and redevelopment of areas that occurred over time. Peculiar enough, it is a treasure in a commercialized area, sitting right on Route 27 just off highway 95 and at the forefront of the Residence Inn Marriott.

Mr. Dudley Woodbridge seemed to have the mansion built as a home for him and his wife to live out their final twenty years. Mr. Woodbridge passed in 1790 and his wife, Sarah, in 1796, long after they had made quite a mark on the property, having raised some of their younger children there. One of the youngest children, born in 1758, passed away just after moving into the home in the early 1770s. He was only about twelve years old and did not get to enjoy too much of his time there. The other children grew

Whitehall Mansion, circa 1980. *Photo courtesy of the Mystic River Historical Society, Inc., Mystic, Connecticut.*

up to get married and move to surrounding areas, with the exception of the second youngest daughter, Lucy. Lucy remained unmarried, and it is believed she spent her time in the home with her parents all the way through to their passing. When Dr. Woodbridge and Sarah had both passed in 1796, it was evident that neither left a will, and a local court appointed two of Dudley's sons, Samuel and William, as executors of the estate. We must remember that in this day, a woman or daughter would not automatically be given executor rights if there were elder males in the family. The eldest son, William, was a Yale graduate like his father and as the eldest was given a double share in the estate, including the main home. Though he and his wife, Zerviah, inherited the property as a couple, they did not reside there and they had no children, which means no immediate family members were living at the home during their ownership. William lived to be eighty years old, and his wife, who was only sixty-eight at his passing, survived for several years after his death. She benefited greatly from his will, still not, however, receiving or moving into the Whitehall Mansion.

Although Dudley's wife was there until her passing in 1796, it remains unclear who lived there for the years that the property belonged to William and Zerviah. There is speculation that Dudley's son Joseph was very close with his brother William and that he, his wife and daughter Lucy occupied the house, leaving it to their descendants. Lucy married her cousin William Rodman, who was the son of Dudley's daughter Elizabeth and her husband, Daniel Rodman. This would make some chronological and common sense since the Rodmans went on to inherit the property upon William Woodbridge's death.

Some historians are curious about a man named Jared Wilcox whose name was etched into the wall of the milk house on the property and suspect that he may have lived there with his wife. Most of this is based on town gossip, however, and there were no property records indicating his tenancy and certainly not indicating ownership.

For all intents and purposes, the property was passing through the family lines as expected, but now with Zerviah and William, the proper hierarchy seemed in question.

When William Woodbridge died in 1825, the property passed to his nephews, William Rodman, son of his sister Elizabeth, and nephew William H. Woodbridge, son of his brother Joseph. Two grandnephews on the Rodman side also stood to share their piece of the property with their dad. William Rodman, married to his cousin and Woodbridge's niece Lucy, had five children, one of whom died in infancy at an undisclosed time. Two of his other children, Daniel and Thomas, were the ones who inherited the property with their father and uncle. Their uncle William Woodbridge only held on to his property interest for twelve years before officially signing it over to his brother-in-law and the Rodman boys. Many believe the Rodman boys added what is known as the ell on to the mansion.

There seem to be so many Williams that it is hard to keep track, but to be sure, each one and their families left their own significant footprint on Whitehall Mansion, both physically and spiritually.

William Rodman, the grandnephew of the first William Woodbridge and son of the first William Rodman, was also a Yale graduate, keeping with the trend of highly educated occupants of the mansion. His time at Whitehall was brief before he pursued his medical practices in other areas of Connecticut and he sold his share of the Whitehall property in 1845 to his brothers Daniel and Thomas just a year after their dad sold his share to Daniel and Thomas as well. Thus, Daniel and Thomas became the sole owners of the estate. Oddly enough, the actual occupants of the mansion during this era remain a mystery. Daniel went off to study at Yale and pursued ministry in other parts of Connecticut while his brother Thomas studied at Yale Medical School and pursued his medical profession as well in alternate parts of the Nutmeg State. Most believe that though the property belonged to the sons, their parents lived there until their passing, and their mother, Lucy, was indeed documented to have passed away in the Whitehall Mansion years later.

As if Whitehall's familial lineage isn't confusing enough, yet another family named the Wheelers was brought into the mix when a farmer named Joseph Wheeler purchased the property in 1852 and moved in with his wife, Mary, and their two daughters, aged four and six at the time. Their third child, another daughter, was born in Whitehall. The place was once again bustling with familial energy, particularly the energy of growing young women. Sadly, many believed their father had some kind of curse or bad luck during his time at Whitehall. Poor Joseph plowed part of the Whitehall Cemetery ground up during his farming ventures, disturbing a great many residents and ancestors and requiring him to rebury the graves and repair the land's damage. It was only shortly after this that Joseph fell ill with consumption and took off to Florida, completely abandoning his farming career. He returned to Connecticut sometime later, and just ten years after his acquisition of the Whitehall property, he and the family moved out of the home to another residence in Mystic. Joseph passed just ten years after this in 1872. He had still owned the estate at the time of his death, but it remains unclear who lived there between 1862 and 1872.

Many historians and local Mystic residents have suggested that the mansion was actually used as a location for a Connecticut Underground Railroad hiding place, and during that time, the asylum space for slaves en route to freedom was located in the attic of the home. Though we cannot be certain if any of the transients passed away in the home, we do know that the room that harbors the door to the attic seems to give people the chills and the constant sense that there are people up there watching or walking about, as well as a slight sense of fear that something foreboding is coming in the future. Perhaps the Whitehall Mansion still contains the energy of the enslaved, who were running for their lives, consumed by the thought of being caught and either killed or sent back to servitude.

As far as documentation during this tension-riddled era, local papers state that the property was leased for ten years by a man named John R. Babcock and his sister. Perhaps they were of assistance to those on the Underground Railroad and leased the property to aid in their departure. Whatever they used the property for is not documented in property history, thus adding to the thrill of elusiveness and mystery that surrounds certain gaps in Whitehall's history. There are also rumors of slaves, servants and farmhands spending time in the mansion with their families and calling the building home. As a spiritualist and a historian of sorts, I often believe that it is these periods of vague factual evidence with hints of information that produce some of our unnamed yet still very active ghostly residents.

In 1872, when Joseph Wheeler passed, he split the land share among the three daughters in his will. The land had been so divided up that by this time, it only totaled thirty-seven acres, including the mansion house, barn and various other small buildings or sheds. (Joseph Wheeler's bad luck even continued after his passing, for the barn that he had established was struck by lightning and burned to the ground years later in 1905.) One of the three daughters, Louise, had become a schoolteacher and was married to a man named Samuel Bentley, who was the local Mystic postmaster. They ended up residing on the Whitehall property. The Wheeler-Bentleys seemed to carry on the tradition of a female-dominated family and had four girls of their own, who were all brought up on the property and went to lead very successful lives. Matriarch Louise Bentley passed away first in 1900 and left the property directly to her husband and children. Samuel passed ten years later in 1910, when all his daughters were spread around the state on their own ventures, pursuing careers as schoolteachers just like their mother. Daughters Mary and Annie both married and had no children. Daughter Florence married a Yale professor and celebrated her wedding in 1913. Florence and her husband, Dewitt Keach, had two sons. Whitehall was quite the place for nuptial celebrations, dating from the 1600s on, and Florence was just one more in a long line of family daughters who married at the homestead. In the immediate Bentley family alone, Annie married there in 1907, and Mary married years prior to that. Sister Julia never married nor had children.

Florence and her sisters shared the property over the years for vacations and family time while a farmer lived in a rented part of the house. Julia passed early in 1934, Annie in 1959 and Florence's last remaining sister, Mary, deeded her share of the property to Florence in 1960, passing away only three years later. In 1960, Florence Bentley Keach became the last remaining owner of Whitehall Mansion. Since the property had a legacy of ministry and medicine from Yale graduates that led to generations of educators and a continuing tradition at Yale, Florence had a huge piece of history in her hands. Generations of weddings, child rearing, early deaths, farming, cooking and wars were seen by the Whitehall house by the time 1960 rolled around. In 1962, as sole benefactor of the estate, Florence realized what a true gem she had and gave the Whitehall Mansion to the Stonington Historical Society. The historical society foresaw what extreme expense would be brought on by a substantial restoration, but with the support of establishments throughout the Mystic community, it was able to restore the mansion to an astounding glory. On top of this, Interstate 95 was being built right through the Whitehall area, and the home ended up being physically relocated twice to where it currently sits. Some even mention that a fire took part of it after its restoration, leading to even more restoration years later. After proper restoration, the Whitehall Mansion was later sold to the Waterford Hotel Group, which includes Residence Inn Marriott, which is now the keeper of this astounding property. Perhaps the restoration drew some of the spirit activity, or perhaps it was simply the bustling activity that took place over centuries. Regardless, Whitehall's spirits seem to have numerous tales to spin.

Upon entering Whitehall through the back door, you arrive in the living area, inclusive of a quaint fireplace, an area to make coffee, a couple of sofas and a coffee table. It possesses a warm, antique, homey feeling inside. Just above a small breakfast table, there are bookshelves housing journals that document guest experiences over the years. The experiences date back over twenty years, and most start with a thank-you to the innkeepers of years past and present for their hospitality, detailing the warmness and quaintness that they felt during the stay. Oftentimes, guests divulged in the journals some very personal details about a honeymoon or romantic stay. Slowly, accounts begin to appear in journals referencing inexplicable and sometimes frightening sensations or observations during the stay. The bone-chilling accounts progress throughout the journals as paranormal activity seems to become abundantly noticed in the household. As the activity seemed to increase, so, too, did the guests' efforts to debunk the situations or come to some sort of practical reasoning as to why things may be happening in their colonial surroundings.

There are five bedrooms that can be checked out within the inn. Most of the journal entries reveal that initially, most guests believed that it was, in fact, other living people inhabiting other rooms that were creating such noise. One guest reported hearing loud, raucous laughter of a woman for hours on end. While she and her spouse didn't want to fault anyone for having a grand time on their holiday away, the laughter continued to roar into the evening

Sign at the entrance of the Whitehall Mansion Inn.

hours when the guests wanted nothing more than to go to sleep. Finally, the tired guests called into the Residence Inn Marriott and asked if the front desk could make a call to the other room in the inn where the laughter was emanating from and ask them to please quiet down since others were trying to sleep. The receptionist was fairly certain but after double-checking the reservations log just to be sure, he informed the perturbed couple that they were the only guests staying in the inn. There was simply no one to call. Promptly, the couple requested that they be compensated with a room inside the Residence Inn Marriott and out of the Whitehall Mansion. They claimed that there was no way they could be expected to stay there after it was revealed that they were the only people checked into the inn, yet there was clearly the audible sound of others there. The hotel obliged, and the guests raced away to a more modern and less ghostly setting.

The sound of others in the inn seems to be a common complaint. Children are not allowed to stay in the inn due to the older nature of the floors and the building itself not really being conducive to housing playful kids. Therefore, it is mostly couples and sometimes the lone traveler who stay in the inn. Another couple again heard laughter, but this was not that of a woman. They distinctly heard children running around giggling as if playing in the inn. Wanting to inform the hotel staff of the disturbance, the couple grabbed the phone in their room and tried to ring the front desk at the Residence Inn. To their dismay, their phone was dead. Though they thought it strange, they decided to call from their mobile phone, which could not be found anywhere. After much searching, they found their mobile phone under the center of their bed. Repeatedly, they dialed the phone to no avail, and they kept getting disconnected. After dialing three times, they finally were connected to the desk. When they finally reached the attendant and found out that they were the only guests staying in the inn, they, too, promptly ran over to the Residence Inn, leaving the room in disarray and requesting more modern and ghost-free lodging.

The rooms are all named for the original Dudley Woodbridge children and his wife, and there are experiences throughout all the rooms. Often the journals will divulge which room has what activity. Betsey's room, for instance, houses the locked door to the attic believed to have once harbored an Underground Railroad location that gives guests an uneasy or fearful feeling. Lucy's room hosts the giggling children who play pranks on their guests and move furniture. Benjamin's room (named after the child who passed away in the inn) has a more somber tone and sometimes just a sheet tug or the feeling of being watched. Sarah's room has a clear motherly

Whitehall Mansion Inn, circa 2014.

presence and is usually the room where guests feel safe. Though guests feel safe in Sarah's quarters, this room, along with the Woodbridge Hall, still possesses a variety of activity indicating watchful spirits.

Different employees from the Marriott who look over the inn have varying contacts with the spirits. Some embrace its spooky appeal, while others have spent the night in various rooms not experiencing anything too alarming but not feeling quite alone either. An assistant manager informed me that when he was in Betsey's room with the door leading to the attic, he had the most uncomfortable feeling that the door would move or there would be sounds above him throughout the evening. Is this perhaps the sounds of individuals escaping dire straights in Southern slavery and captivity? Finally, there are others, particularly housekeepers, who are asked to enter the home on a regular basis who often flee with some kind of fear after a noise or inexplicable movement. They also claim that there are certain doors that always reopen, even when locked, and often they have to do double or triple checks.

A common assertion for staff and guests alike is the feeling that the pictures on the walls are in fact watching your every move. If you look carefully or perhaps out of the corner of your eye, you can see the eyes in all the antique portraits literally moving to follow your movements. Many guests admit that the sensation of being watched is so strong that they take down the photos during their stay and face them toward the wall before they attempt a peaceful slumber. They just could not get rid of the feeling that the person in the photo was looking right at them.

Sometimes guests will see a light flicker and think perhaps it's some old wiring or hear a board creak and assume it's probably just the fact that the house is old, but other times, when it is followed by a faint giggle or the sound of scampering feet, they can't help but wonder what else it could be. This happens a great deal in Lucy's room, where guests walk into the adjoining bathroom only to emerge and see that a table or chair has moved clear across the room or that the bedsheets have been turned down.

As a Halloween special for the haunted excursions in Mystic, I had the good fortune of being able to give a tour in the Whitehall Mansion. When doing so, we did a walk-through of each and every room, giving our tour goers a unique spin with tales centered on each place they stood. Lucy's room was our final stop on the tour as it is considered to be the most active spot where children are most often heard. Prior to the tour, I did a walk-through with one of the managerial employees who was quite fun-loving and supportive of our venture. He informed me that staff has had to check doors and prop them open or secure them shut as things sometimes moved, but otherwise, he had never had a very frightening experience. Everything seemed calm on the front in our pre-tour walk-through, and the tour itself was going quite smoothly. When we went to enter Lucy's room, the door was a bit hard to open. It wasn't all the way open, as we had left it. When we entered, we realized a table had been pushed almost up against the door. Before the guests came in, I asked our friend and employee of the inn if he had noticed that the table had moved or if he had come back up in the room. He looked at me for a second, kind of puzzled, and assured me that he had not moved that table and that he could vouch that it wasn't there before. We, of course, excitedly and nervously shared the story with our guests and admitted that we never quite expected in our ninety minutes within the home that the ghosts would grace us with such an active display of their antics. At the same time, it was rather nice to have that confirmation of the haunted truth within Whitehall Mansion.

Whoever the lively spirits are, they do not approve of inappropriate or untoward behavior in their home. One man tentatively admitted in the journals that he had come to the inn with his mistress so as not to be caught by his wife. During the committing of adultery, the bedsheets were tugged and the man was painfully pinched in the leg. He said the experience was so shocking that his heart almost stopped, and he vowed in that journal to never cheat again. In this same bed, another man who wrote that he, too, was with his female companion had his leg lifted into midair and held there for some time. Who he was with remains unclear, but perhaps the ghost in Benjamin's room is keeping an eye on who is betrothed properly and who is not before they enter into that bed.

Benjamin Woodbridge was the child who passed in the home and many spiritualists—including my own mother—still feel the sensation that his namesake bedroom is likely also the room in which he passed. There is a bit of sadness to the room, more the sadness of a parent, and perhaps it's the parent watching over the adults who come into her child's room without proper respect and acknowledgement.

Young Benjamin Woodbridge and all other children, adults and even some slaves or servants who spent a part of their time in the Whitehall Mansion are quietly in their resting place at the Whitehall Burial Ground. This is situated across the street behind a local hardware store. It's a small burial ground with gatherings of stones in each family name, including Gallup, Woodbridge, Rodman and more. There are some other family stones in there as well. As you walk through the grounds, you will be visiting nearly all of the owners and tenants of the Whitehall Mansion over the past three hundred years.

The small cemetery dates back to the times of the original landowners, the aforementioned Gallups. In 1754, a deed attributed to William Gallup established a parcel of land "that the neighbors thereabout might enjoy the Burying Place forever." Many Gallups from the Mystic Country were laid to rest in this peaceful plot, and erected hundreds of years ago, there also sits a monument to Captain John Gallup, who was killed in the Great Swamp Fight of Captain Phillip's War.

An article from the New London–area newspaper the *Day* indicated in 1997 that the care of the burying ground was provided for by a benefactor with the goal of maintaining the look of a colonial-style burying place. In fact, some of the antique, dated and fine carvings on these stones can only be seen in other areas of New England with well-preserved burial spots dating to the 1700s and beyond, such as in Salem, Massachusetts. The *Day*'s article goes on to confirm the unique historical relevance of this tiny burying ground in southeastern Connecticut. Reporter Carol Kimball detailed the historical relevance spanning the decades of the burying place, writing, "Whitehall embodies much significant American history, for it is the final resting place

Whitehall burial ground gated entrance, circa 2014. *Photo by Shelby McInvale.*

Whitehall burial ground. *Photo by Shelby McInvale.*

Burial monument to Captain John Gallup, killed in the Great Swamp Fight of Captain Phillip's War in 1675. *Photo by Shelby McInvale.*

of many Afro-Americans, including the lay preacher Quash, and other freed slaves. The yard also has had a number of Native American burials, some of them in recent years from the Mashantucket (Pequot) tribe."

There is a sad feeling in the cemetery, and many locals have gotten pictures of orbs or sworn they saw someone walking through, only to vanish in front of them as they pay their respects to the Mystic elders of yore. When I was doing some research, I chose to take a walk through the burying ground on my own and was even able to capture a disembodied voice on an audio recorder I had turned on purely for curiosity.

If you're heading down to the river for a weekend away, it might be fun to take a step back in time to the canopied beds, the rustic fireplaces, the beautiful modern amenities and spa-like tubs that the Whitehall Mansion offers, and if you're a paranormal buff, you may just catch some supernatural action on your stay. It's a beautiful and historic marker of what New England homesteads and mansions used to be, and it's a place that its previous residents can't help but come back to. You'll take note of the larger and perhaps grander Elmwood Cemetery just down the way from Whitehall Mansion's current placement, but when you're around, take a short stroll through the more secluded Whitehall Burying Ground as well to give your regards to all who stayed in that building and on that land so long before any of us. Natives, slaves and prominent Mystic citizens all rest together on Whitehall land. When you pay a visit to the historic homestead, you may also feel compelled to pen your experiences in the journals for future guests to read. Above all, know that Whitehall Mansion is a place of both mystery and comfort. The charm therein lies within that paradox.

Chapter 4

New England Traditions of History, Hospitality, Fine Dining and Ghostly Guests

Old Mystic Inn

It was a cold, winter evening just before Christmas in 1999 when Michael Cardillo Jr. first settled into his newly acquired inn. Michael went to bed excited, his head spinning with thoughts about the beautiful property he had recently purchased. With his brand-new inn, he would be able to pass down New England traditions of food, hospitality and legendary folklore that had spanned generations. He'd be able share with visitors from around the world an authentic feeling of home in quiet and scenic southeastern Connecticut. What better place to create a hospitable stay for the incoming guests than in an eighteenth-century center-chimney colonial homestead with Victorian additions?

The incoming wintry chill, fitting for the holiday season, had set just long enough in the air for Michael to have garnered numerous stacks of wood. He kept them piled against the stone wall paralleling the attached porch alongside the house. As the new innkeeper, he had made sure that he was fully prepared to fuel the fireplaces throughout the inn while guests sipped on hot tea and read their favorite novels. A truly picturesque scene would come when the snow began to fall. As he laid his head down on the pillow, putting his busy and excited mind to rest, Michael eventually found himself finally in a deep sleep. Hours passed, and in the middle of the night, Michael began to scream. The screams became blood-curdling, clearly indicating some kind of pure horror. His mother, who had been visiting for the evening, ran immediately to his aid. Finally, she was able to wake him out of what she could only assume was a most terrifying nightmare.

As Michael awoke, he began to explain what he had envisioned: a woman appearing totally in white, clothed in colonial-era dress was standing by the wood piles that he had stacked outside the inn. He couldn't look away, and there she stood, looking him in the eye, staring back at him silently, as if to say, "Welcome to my home."

Just over the river and up the road from the downtown area is what is now known as Old Mystic. As anyone local will kindly remind you, though, Old Mystic was the first Mystic. When the "new" downtown area developed and Mystic's population grew commensurately, the first settlement of Mystic was adequately renamed. By 1890, the new identity had been assumed, and the first Mystic had become known as Old Mystic. Old Mystic has a general store, churches, old schoolhouse sites, playgrounds and bed-and-breakfasts or local inns aplenty. River Road runs into Old Mystic, providing a summertime hangout for artists, kayakers and the like. With its very own Old World charm as you drive through the village, your eyes will be drawn straight away to the historical ambience within all the residences and small inns.

What we now know is that as time continually elapses, there are more and more people leaving their imprints on the buildings and land that they'll inevitably leave behind. This inherently gives each structure and landscape an indescribable character of its own. Oftentimes, some visitors or residents from decades before come by in their ghostly form to check on their old homestead, visit a loved one or perhaps clear up some unfinished business. They simply can't help but be brought back to the house they left behind.

An inn in Old Mystic aptly named the Old Mystic Inn sits in an antiquated homestead colored a deep crimson red, almost that of brick. The house dates all the way back to before the turn of the nineteenth century and was built in 1784 by John Denison. At the time of its construction, Denison had the home built purely for speculation. The house underwent some rapid changes of hands, going to John's son Nathan by 1785 and then to Nathan's brother-in-law John Baldwin in 1789. The house stayed within some circles of the Denison family and the Williams family for the next thirty-six years.

By the time 1804 rolled around, the house may have acquired one of its most mysterious residents to date in Ms. Lucy Williams. Not much is known about Ms. Lucy Williams herself. However, when she passed away in 1825, her will was so remarkably strange that all those who read its dictation to this very day are completely baffled as to what goal she had when she left the property so awkwardly divided up in her final documents. Lucy bequeathed the Main Street property as follows: "From the north to the south 5 feet 11

Old Mystic Inn as a historic homestead, circa 1895–1915. *Photo courtesy of Michael Cardillo Jr., the Old Mystic Inn.*

inches wide to 5 feet 2 inches wide, then six people to have shares in the dwelling house to extend from the roof to the ground three feet three inches wide." Some of those who stood to inherit portions of property and space in the dwelling house include other members of the Williams family, the Babcock family, the Hewitt family and more. Eventually, all of dear Lucy's heirs sold their shares to the Denison and Brown families, and the rest of the building's tenancy appears to have gone without curious divisiveness. The property eventually returned back to being titled as one entity.

During the midst of all these property-sharing landowners, a structure was built on what is now the Old Mystic Inn's property corner. Through records belonging to prominent Mystic resident of years past Mr. Charles Eldredge, we gain a picturesque perspective. At the exact time this apportionment of land was selected for its new purpose, it had been sitting just south of the Hyde Estate. Mr. Hyde had thirteen children and seemed quite motivated to acquire an education facility for them in his hometown. The new structure of much discussion would serve as the primary educational establishment for children of the community. Officially, on April 24, 1839, a portion of the now Old Mystic Inn's property was granted to the Sixth School District in the Village of Mystic, town of Stonington. Much like the name of the community changed to Old Mystic in 1890, so did the name of the school change to the Sixth School District in the Village of Old Mystic, town of Stonington. Though titled the Sixth School District, it was in fact the very first school to be built in Old Mystic.

Eldredge's letter from January 1930 provided yet more detail, continuing that originally the schoolhouse served all ages and grades and actually originally stood at first as a simple one-room schoolhouse, as was commonly seen throughout New England. However, Mr. Eldredge's accounts show that by 1851, the school had become a two-story building, and students who passed their classes with high aptitude and skill graduated from the ground level to the second level. A newer school was built around the 1870s or 1880s just to the north of this one and expanded to four rooms. This would have sat on what would now be regarded as the backside of the Old Mystic Inn property. The original schoolhouse became a family home for about thirty years before it was lost tragically to yet another Mystic fire in the early 1900s. The larger and more improved schoolhouse expanded some and remained an educational structure in Old Mystic until 1959, when overcrowding prevented these smaller schoolhouses from being adequate any longer to a growing population and importance placed on education. A new brick school was built in 1959, and the antiquated Sixth School District in the

Old Mystic Playground sign, circa 2014.

Village of Mystic saw its end. This third school eventually also could not serve the growing populations of the Mystic community, and a new school was built. The third schoolhouse became an administrative building for the local board of education.

The playground that was established where the second schoolhouse had once been still sits behind the property and is fondly called the Old Mystic Playground. Indeed, the story goes that the playground comes with some spirits of its very own, perhaps inherited from the property's many years housing the local schools.

The schoolhouse's geographic removal from the Old Mystic Inn area did not happen without leaving at least one mystery to fit in well with paranormal legends that surround it. In 1877, the Meneely Bell Foundry had provided a 198-pound bell for the second schoolhouse, located where the playground now sits. The *Mystic River Press* reported on the bell in 1877, saying that it had "a much better tone than the 'cow bell' which has hitherto called the scholars to their daily tasks." Over the years, the bell became a revered item for schoolchildren as it was considered a big honor to be the selected student who rang the bell at the end of the day. Of course, as the twentieth century plowed forward, pranks were also held in high regard, and many students loved to break into the school on Halloween night and ring the bell at the first stroke of the midnight hour. All of this was in good fun—until the bell seemingly disappeared. After the schoolhouse was vacated, records don't indicate where the bell may have gone. Some believe it could have been melted down and recast, while others are certain that a bell of that size, magnitude and historical importance was likely taken by someone who wanted to preserve it as a treasure.

The Old Mystic community asked anyone with information on the bell to come forward, but the bell has never been found and no one seems to know where this nearly two-hundred-pound item could be hiding. Could it be tied to a ghostly presence? We can't be sure, as that's an awfully large item to go missing at the hands of a ghost, yet it would not be the first time that the spirits have had their fun causing items to go missing. The mystery lives on, and so does the spirit activity at the Old Mystic Inn, on the inn's property where the schoolhouse once sat and beyond. So, let's move forward to some more history of this inn just around the bend.

As years passed, the main house on the property where the tourist favorite now sits saw varying families well known in the local Mystic community of yore move in and out of the house. In the 1920s, the William Harvey family resided in the home while it was in hand of Benton Copp, an owner of many properties throughout town. Sometimes the home— which was such a large size for the turn of the twentieth century and even earlier—served as a multi-family home. In fact, in the early to late 1930s, additional Williams family members resided in the house. Mr. and Mrs. Frank Williams moved into the home, along with Mr. and Mrs. Kenneth Williams, who lived on the second floor.

World War II came quickly, and after nearly four years, wartime for America came to a close. It was a long and harsh time for many in the country, and as such, properties often fell into disregard and were not extremely well kept. Basic information regarding changing of hands was documented, but that would usually be where the property card ended. In the 1940s, the Old Mystic home was sold to the Metznacher family, and a woman named Alberta White Storm recalls living there in the mid-1950s while her husband was deployed with the military. She distinctly remembered the wallpaper that remained inside for many years even after her brief residency.

By 1959, the home no longer served as a primary residence. Mr. Charles Vincent owned the property and utilized the home to run a bookstore. The bookstore operated for almost twenty-five years, ending in 1986. Residents who recall visiting the bookstore said that every room on the ground floor was jam-packed with books from floor to ceiling almost to the point that you could barely walk in the establishment. Mr. Vincent himself, however, knew his collection so well that he could find any book you were there to inquire about. The legacy of Charles Vincent and his bookstore lives on at the property to this day. The artistic etching that is on the sign reading Old Mystic Inn displayed at the front of the home for all travelers to see was made in the likeness of Charles himself. Beyond that, all of the guest rooms are named after well-known and beloved classic authors, inspired by the home's history and the plethora of books it once housed.

Mr. Vincent sold the property, and it changed hands to the owners who established the home as an inn. After many renovations, the new lodging house in Old Mystic opened its doors in June 1987, and the accompanying Carriage House, providing even more accommodations, was built on the property and opened in 1988.

The inn changed hands once more before it was finally sold in 1999 to the present owner, who has turned the Old Mystic Inn into the beloved home away from home for travelers and tourists across the world who visit the Mystic Country today.

When Michael Cardillo Jr. purchased the property in 1999, he was well prepared to carry on the tradition of being the innkeeper of such a coveted

The Old Mystic Inn's entrance sign, depicting the former owner of the site's bookshop, Charles Vincent.

and lovely establishment. Cardillo, a professionally trained chef, has thrilled many a Mystic traveler with their local experience, including great food, a historic home and the bustling activities of the community at their fingertips. Traveler testimonials can't rave enough about the hospitality, graciousness and historic beauty that the property possesses.

Some, though, including Michael and his friend Robert Lecce Jr., can't help but notice the frequent presence or energy from some of the more ghostly guests over years past.

Working with historical societies and town halls, it quickly becomes evident that death records for specific homes are harder to come by than one might imagine. Many death records will indicate when a person died and what properties they owned, but rarely will death records be marked with statements such as "She/he died in her bed at home," or "she/he died of suicide in her own home." Many times, unless a victim passed away in a tragic homicide or unfortunate newsworthy disaster where documentation would be kept by reporters or other tenants, any other type of homeowner or resident death within their own property of natural causes, accident or suicide would be recorded with a simple date and time. Occasionally, especially in more recent years, an obituary may be easier to find. This is again limiting in facts (and rightfully so) by the information that loved ones elect to provide. That leaves us as researchers in a peculiar place when it comes to deaths in an eighteenth-century property. We can only speculate with some help from property records and occasionally help from a well-respected psychic-medium to what specific types of deaths may have happened in or around this property and who just may not be ready to leave it behind.

The Old Mystic Inn has strange occurrences aplenty. Though for most we are unable to pinpoint an exact name, we can be sure that active spirits have made themselves known in appearance, sound and in the dreams of those who sleep there.

Since Michael Cardillo Jr.'s dream, he hasn't laid eyes on any apparitions around the inn, but there are often sounds and inexplicable movements that he simply can't dismiss. Never feeling endangered, he goes about his business of operating the inn with his friendly spirits likely watching over with nods of approval. Michael's good friend Robert has sometimes seen the ghostly images of those spirits who make their way around the house, and a friend of Robert's with psychic abilities has also been able to see some of these spirits as well. To add even more compelling evidence of paranormal entities in abundance at the inn, there are guests who have reported their own sightings in the dead of the night, and a paranormal investigation group spent an evening at the inn and left with numerous audio recordings of spirit voices and photographic evidence.

As aforementioned, Michael is a great chef and graduated from the Culinary Institute of America, so when guests stay at the inn, he can usually be found preparing a scrumptious breakfast in the kitchen during the early hours of the morning. One morning, as he was standing at the counter preparing breakfast, his friend Robert, who had been assisting in the kitchen, caught sight of something shocking. As Robert moved to the side of the kitchen, a person appeared in his peripheral vision, stopping him dead in his tracks. What he saw was the silhouette of a woman in colonial attire with the traditional tight-fitted waist standing on the opposite side of the counter watching quite closely as Michael cooked. She appeared almost as if she wanted to get more involved herself in the food prep and cooking that was taking place. Robert stood there, mouth agape, and completely bewildered. At first, he was unsure what to say when Michael noticed him standing there and naturally asked why he looked so confused.

"Are you kidding me, Michael?" Robert nervously laughed. How had Michael not seen her standing right in front of him? Immediately, Robert began to explain what he had witnessed. He described in detail that a woman adorned in colonial-style clothing, middle-aged or older, was standing there watching them cook. Michael tried to brush it off, not wanting to be scared in his own kitchen, yet it didn't seem surprising to hear. He knew the history of the home was vast and there were always strange noises happening about. What if it was the lady in white from his dream? If so, he definitely knew who she was!

Robert called his friend with psychic abilities so that she could visit the inn and perhaps pick up more information regarding the lady in the kitchen or any other spirits that may be there. When the psychic arrived in the kitchen, a smile overcame her face. She had immediately sensed the colonial woman's presence. After focusing for a bit, the psychic let Michael know that the kitchen's spirit had some culinary advice. She had wanted to use more fresh herbs and spices and put grated nutmeg over eggnog, and the list carried on. Clearly, this colonial woman—whose name is believed to have begun with H, according to the psychic-medium—had her opinions about proper cuisine and even had suggestions for the most well-trained chefs. On a more somber note, it was reported during the psychic's contact that the colonial woman was waiting for a loved one to come home, yet they never could. Her loved one likely drowned in the Mystic River, as did so many hundreds of years ago when numerous people had no ability to swim. Before the colonial woman's communication with the psychic ceased, she made sure to ask that a chair be placed back by the kitchen table rather than a hutch, as she would like to sit there. It seems she'd like to watch the cooking, as this may have been her favorite endeavor in life. The colonial woman brings no harm, just a warm heart and some suggestions for a good meal while she waits in her eternity for a loved one to come home. Guests who have reported sightings of a lady in white roaming around, not really bothering anyone but just checking in, may have just seen the colonial chef. Perhaps, though, it's one of the many other spirits roaming about the land.

The psychic was able to sense more of the numerous spirits that call the Old Mystic Inn home. Sadly, she reported that a man still roams around the inn who had likely once hanged himself in the home. He had actually been a clammer of quahogs in his life. The man is also harmless to guests and to the owners. He simply seems to exude extreme sadness, sometimes roaming about the hall searching for the answers to painful questions. He likely sought to have this search ended in the afterlife, but alas, it seems that it was not ended and the gentleman is still searching for a way to complete his unfinished business. The intuitives who have visited the inn have envisioned hanging feet from the ceiling of one of the rooms implying a suicide may have occurred in the home. Others may feel sadness or darkness when he is nearby, perhaps in his former bedroom. Some visitors, particularly those who are intuitive, feel that one guest room in particular may have at one time been his primary residence or bedroom, as he can often be felt or sometimes seen sitting on the bed with hands on his head, almost rocking back and forth trying to decide how to move forward. One guest even reported sighting him from the doorway, watching ever so closely as he thought they were sleeping. This gave her a bit of a fright, but she sensed no ill will from the man. Some mediums have even felt a pressure on their necks, possibly confirming that a suicide by hanging was indeed a tragic event that took place in the house at one time.

The Old Mystic Inn has also been the subject of investigations and ghost hunts from local Connecticut groups. These investigations have subsequently resulted in some interesting findings, evidence and corroboration of what psychic-mediums have detected. A highlight for both psychics and ghost hunters who visit the old homestead on Main Street is the detection of child spirits. One medium suggested the presence of an eight-year-old child called Hannah in the home and numerous other younger spirits that visit on a regular basis. Hannah's activities reportedly include sitting on her favorite stool and playing until she accidentally falls off and hoop rolling around the property. Hoop trundling was a game very popular in early to mid-1800s America. Hannah's affinity for hoop rolling perhaps gives us a time frame for when she may have lived or attended school on the property. Another psychic-medium suggested that a young boy who drowned nearby in the Mystic River or perhaps the closer Whitford Brook frequently visits as well. Having once had a schoolhouse on the property and still harboring a playground in the backyard, it stands to reason that spirits of children would definitely be drawn to this particular property.

When local ghost hunters descended on the property, they tried to communicate with the children and whoever else might be visiting the home as a spirit entity. The local ghost hunters investigated the home, the property and the playground and tried to speak with any resident spirits throughout those areas. Their recording devices picked up some interesting results on their EVP (electronic voice phenomena) recorders. When the investigators were standing in the playground area, they immediately noticed that the EVP recorders had picked up the sounds of two voices. They heard the voices repeating in frantic, hushed tones, "Help me! Help Me!" After time elapsed and no additional significant EVPs were captured at the playground, the paranormal researchers made their final inquiry to the spirits at the playground and inquired if they were welcome to return. A disembodied voice responded back with a loud and resounding "No." That didn't seem typical for a child to say, and it did not sound like a child's voice, either. Was some type of adult who may have harmed children or perhaps a demon keeping these children or others trapped in the playground? Who was screaming, "Help Me"? It is hard to say without knowing who the children may be, but it is certain that children did die in the area; schoolhouses did once sit there and psychic-mediums have picked up on young boy, young girl and adult spirits on the property of the Old Mystic Inn.

With such abundant spirit activity, there is likely a plethora of individuals haunting their old homestead or school grounds. Some ghostly entities, be them children or adults, that have named themselves in paranormal investigations or to a psychic-medium are Darrel, Nathan, Jeremy, Godfrey and Ezra. These are quite a variety of names, to be sure, and some of them typical old English first names likely found often in the early Connecticut settlements. Property records do indeed indicate that a Nathan Denison owned the property around the turn of the nineteenth century, which can perhaps account for the spirit called Nathan. Perhaps the property owner himself or a child called by his name is one of the spirits who call the inn home. In fact, another EVP recording at the property captured the voice of a woman with a distinct Irish accent stating, "I thought Nathan was here." Even fellow spirits are looking for the Old Mystic's Inn resident ghost named Nathan. Other EVP snippets captured varying voices. One inquired, "Are you a policeman?" to the ghost hunting crews. Another remarked, "That's a vehicle." Others were more inviting and actually said, "Come on in" as if they were opening the door for their guests. Some audio recordings revealed the sounds of joyful laughter, clearly indicating the harmless and maybe even fun-loving natures of so many of the spirits at the Old Mystic Inn.

Rest assured, you need not be a seasoned ghost hunter or psychic-medium to have a sighting or sensation of your own at the Old Mystic Inn or the surrounding property. Sometimes the spirits are just going about their business, and you may just get a glimpse back in time or hear them passing through. One day while Michael and his friend Robert were in the home doing some work downstairs and talking, they heard one of the guests in the room above them. A nice couple had been staying during the week. The man had left to attend some business meetings, and his wife seemed to have gone out briefly to do some shopping in the morning. Naturally, upon hearing the footsteps above their heads, Michael and Robert assumed that the woman had finished her outing and had come back to spend some of her day at the inn or perhaps take a rest. The footsteps continued for some time, but neither the innkeeper nor his friend took notice for long. It's an older house, and it's inevitable that you hear people walking above you on the old wooden floors. About an hour or so later, the lady entered the inn, said hello to Robert and Michael and walked up to her room. Michael and Robert looked at each other, stunned. They were the only guests in the inn, and if she wasn't walking around up there all this time, who was?

The Old Mystic Inn seems to be quite the spiritual gathering place, almost like a portal to the other side filled with spirits of children, tormented souls, opinionated colonial cooks and more. While some of them could likely have been owners, residents, schoolchildren or locals with some attachment to the property, other locals suggest that they have a distinct idea who at least one of the several ghosts may be. A man named Don Defosses, who used to reside at the former Wayside Inn next door, told Michael and other owners the tale of Margaret Dart, a beautiful young blonde woman who lived across the street from the two inns in the 1950s to 1960s. On the night before Thanksgiving sometime in the beginning of the 1960s, a fire took over her house and burned the structure nearly to the ground with Margaret inside. Margaret could have only been in her mid-twenties at the time, and some suggest that it is her spirit who wanders through the inns of Mystic, including

Old Mystic Inn, circa 2014.

the Old Mystic Inn. Additionally, some rumors say that she is perhaps the "woman in white" so many guests claim to see.

Be it Margaret, British colonial settlers, Puritans, Civil War veterans or playful schoolchildren all the spirits seem to be friendly as far as the innkeeper, his friends and the psychics are concerned. Guests continue to rave about their experience in the antique homestead, feeling a sense of belonging, enjoying delicious food and rating their overall experience as simply exquisite. If guests do catch a glimpse of a spiritual guest passing by, they never report being alarmed, mostly just interested and perhaps feeling a little watched.

The Old Mystic Inn seems to provide safe harbor for guests of both the earthly and spiritual realms, and what more could be asked from a quintessential New England bed-and-breakfast establishment? Be assured as a guest that you will receive top-notch cuisine, peaceful accommodations and gracious hospitality—and if you're extremely lucky, you may get to see a full-bodied apparition.

Chapter 5

SOME SPIRITS JUST CAN'T STOP WORKING

VOODOO GRILL AND THE FACTORY SQUARE

As you turn the corner from the bustling West Main Street filled with little shops and the iconic Mystic Pizza restaurant, you arrive on Water Street, arguably the most haunted corridor in the downtown area and filled with restaurants to suit every palate. The Factory Square block hosts some of these restaurants. Factory Square houses Chinese, Mexican and good 'ol American food with a Cajun twist à la the Voodoo Grill. The rest of the towering brick structures have a couple small offices, an art gallery and condominiums galore. With the rustic look provided by an antique red brick edifice, the buildings are timeless. Though a bit weathered, they are as strong and sturdy as they ever have been. Factory Square was built, of course, to house an industrial complex where hundreds of workers could both create and utilize large pieces of machinery that would be shipped across the nation. Some of the equipment assembled would have been necessary for seafaring people throughout New England, while others were utilized prior to and during wartimes from the Civil War era all the way through World War II. Factory Square, though now purely commercial and residential, was once a bustling workplace, a place of creation, blood, sweat, tears, hard work and decades of evolving machinery. It may not catch your eye at first, but the brick façade and the strength of the structure brings a special piece of history to downtown Mystic and is an integral part of the downtown atmosphere. Factory Square also provides sanctuary to numerous residents of the paranormal persuasion.

Factory worker with horse and cart at Standard Machinery Company, 1904. *Photo from the Dickinson Collection, courtesy of the Mystic River Historical Society, Inc., Mystic, Connecticut.*

As with many historic American factories, official records of accidents and deaths were far from well kept. Factory workers were of the blue-collar and working-class social groups. Thus, any unfortunate happening related to them would not be considered newsworthy. When it came to the Reliable Machine Company, later known as the Standard Machinery Company where Factory Square now sits on Water Street, we can naturally assess that it fell into the norm of many factories in the Industrial Revolution and beyond, causing some employees to succumb to life-threatening injuries. The factory buildings were in business for nearly two hundred years, with workers coming in and out every day on the riverfront creating cotton gin machinery, bookbinding machinery and more.

The first of varying operations that took hold there began in the mid-1850s, just before tensions between the North and South had begun to rise. A man named Isaac Randall who went on to build and own the building known as the former Emporium on Water Street actually operated the factory known in the 1850s and early 1860s as the Reliance Machine Company. During this time, the company manufactured cotton gin machinery and supplies necessary for the Southern market. This was indicative of a still somewhat thriving economy in our growing nation. Times changed rapidly, however, and throughout the Civil War, the Reliance Machine Company also began to furnish boilers and engines for steamers in the Mystic shipyards. Ultimately and unfortunately, the economical recourse of Southern debtors took its toll, and the factory was sold out to new ownership in 1864.

A man named C.B. Rogers of Norwich took control of the factory, which he renamed the Pequot Company. The factory's time as the Pequot Company was brief, lasting only a year and a half before being sold once again to the Cotton Gin Company. The Cotton Gin Company held on to the factory for a bit longer, just about five years, when the economy once again took its toll in 1871. At this time, the factory was purchased yet again and turned into the Mystic River Hardware Company. The Mystic River Hardware Company had a couple good years in it before another change of name was to take place. The one element that remained steadfast throughout all this change was the manufacture of one particular equipment line, and that was cotton gin machinery. During the Mystic River Hardware Company's ownership, the factory added a new long-lasting product to its repertoire with the fabrication of bookbinding machinery. To diversify product even more continuously, the company also manufactured two items that became quite popular in distribution for the late 1800s. These items were known as the Mystic Pump and the People's Improved Coffee Mill.

In 1873, the factory's title was adapted once more, and it became known as the Sanford Machinery Company. It was not long before the factory underwent its final and most long-lasting title and venture that many people in the Mystic community are still familiar with. Under new ownership, the buildings now known as Factory Square became the Standard Machinery Company. Charles Wheeler was the man who acquired the Standard Machinery Company in 1904 and finally modernized a lot of its practices. Wheeler's sons Norton and John joined him in exercising the progress of this modernization. It was during the Wheeler ownership that the company once again evolved and changed its product distribution, halting the creation of bookbinding machinery and beginning the building of molding presses and extruding machines for plastics and rubber industries. The factory remained in use under this repurposing until about 1965, when another factory in neighboring Stonington began to take the bulk of the work.

From 1965 to 1978, the building was not utilized. In 1978, it was purchased by Michael K. Stern of Stern Builders from its owner at that time, Stavros Manousos of Hartford, Connecticut. Stern purchased it having already designed blueprints for Factory Square's huge evolvement into a commercial and housing area, which it remains today. For over two hundred years, the factory served the southeastern Connecticut economy, produced necessary machinery during wartime, created boilers for Mystic steamships and made a mark in the community through its constant development and creation. A place so productive and consistently busy would never be able to let go of all that it has done and all that it has seen, which is why modern-day hauntings seem to abound within it's walls.

Factory Square is unique not only in its large geographical span or grand square footage but also in the fact that it harbors two types of spiritual hauntings, both residual and active. The real-life encounters that residents, visitors and employees report having with Factory Square ghosts depicts occurrences that fit within the molds of both of these haunting natures. The aforementioned history of the factory displays poignantly why both residual and active paranormal occurrences are not just viable but very much existent within the former industrial workplace.

Residual hauntings derive from an area ripe with a particular activity for extended amounts of time. That activity more or less bleeds into the earth. After the earth has inherited that energy from the repeated behavior— whether it is going through the course of business at a factory, serving as a homestead or providing a bed and warm meal for tourists and patrons in an inn—it may still be occurring on just the other side of the veil. For instance, if a building served as a hospital for over one hundred years, the energy of doctors, surgeons and nurses could still exist in that building, regardless of whether they passed away in the hospital. For Factory Square, its history remains within its namesake. Having existed as a factory for over one hundred years, the buildings experienced the day-to-day operations of men, children and possibly some women coming to work and operating heavy equipment and machinery to create various products for local nationwide utilization on land and sea. This energy was absorbed by the building, and through that ever so thin veil, the very same working activity still exists. On occasion, when we as the living, lay our eyes on a ghost, we are actually getting a slight peek back in time through that residual haunting. For a brief moment, it will appear almost as if time can stand still.

An active haunting is one more traditionally thought of and often encountered. Active hauntings can be attributed to individuals, apparitions or activity that seems to relate directly to a circumstance or, more pointedly, to a particular individual's death. A person who passed away in a home is oftentimes the spirit entity or apparition that one encounters in a haunted home. Frequently, the spirit in a home or business can also be that of a deceased person who favored a certain object that the new landowner or resident is currently in possession of. That can also lead to that individual haunting a place. Of course, visitations from a loved one or a spirit drawn to one's aura can bring a more familiar ghostly entity to a residence. An active paranormal spirit is more than just a sneak peek of a ghost that doesn't seem to notice you. Active ghosts are often very coherent of the living in the premises that they are spooking or haunting. For instance, if you are complaining that you have to go to another room to fetch a broom to sweep and the broom seemingly moves across the floor in your direction, one can argue that a spirit aware of its surroundings is present. If you have lost an item and ask where it is, only to have it remarkably appear before your eyes, it can prove that a spirit was playing a funny trick on you. These actions are not considered residual because the entity has proven to be aware of their surroundings. Likely, the ghost is attributed to the history of the land, building or perhaps the individual in the home.

Of all the hauntings I have witnessed, I find Factory Square is the only one where witness accounts and testimonials have provided such compelling evidence of both types of hauntings in one structure. Having been operational

Factory Square, circa 2014.

for nearly two hundred years and specifically having included days prior to the enforcement of safety requirements, it was a busy and active place. Men poured their lives into their work, and sometimes during all this eagerness to generate machinery, occurrences of equipment-related deaths and injuries in such a facility were inevitable and often graphically violent. A lot of times, these types of deaths were swift and pain was not long withstanding. This is one of the main ingredients for a spirit who often doesn't know they have passed. A swift passing can create a sense of confusion for a spirit, though it rarely causes them to be malicious in nature. Thus far, our spirit friends at Factory Square must have been quite the worker bees, for they seem to just be passing through and are nearly always of a nonviolent nature. Admittedly, their activity can, at times, be alarming.

A restaurant and bar located within one of the forefront commercial spaces on Water Street is aptly named Voodoo Grill. From our understanding, Voodoo Grill had its unique name prior to knowing of the ghosts that would come to visit. Be it the spiritual namesake or the location at the forefront of the property, Voodoo Grill of 12 Water Street seems to house many of the Factory Square spirits.

A bartender who has worked at Voodoo Grill for over eight years has had her share of experiences— enough of them to insist that she not work the late hours alone any longer.

One of her first occurrences came as she was working her shift tending bar with one of her colleagues. Everything started as a normal shift, with nothing to remark on as not one thing seemed out of the ordinary. There were a few folks sitting on their barstools, enjoying their New Orleans–themed cocktails and draft beers. No startling sounds or noticeable inconsistencies were present. One of the customers was looking ahead and noticed his eyes drawn to the rack of glasses that sits on the wall behind the bar displayed stem up, cup down. Upon glancing over, he noticed that one of these wine glasses was starting to shift forward on the rack on its own volition, but he didn't remark on the sight. Perhaps his eyes deceived him. He had indulged in a couple of beverages that afternoon, after all. His senses could have been confused, he thought. Sure enough, he quickly learned the beverages were not to blame, and he was not the only one to behold a shocking sight that day. A sudden gasp overcame the customers and bartenders as the glass shifted completely off the wall rack behind it and hovered above the ground for just one or two seconds before it came crashing to the floor. The sounds of breaking glass emanated throughout the establishment. Strangely, however, when everyone looked down, expecting shards of glass to be littering the floor, the fallen

Voodoo Grill, circa 2014.

wine glass was almost completely intact, with just the stem broken off. A mild discussion ensued regarding this. Perhaps there was a small earthquake, or had a big truck gone by? The staff and customers quickly dismissed these thoughts since they heard no truck, the room didn't shake and nothing else moved. Above all else, the glass was not teetering near the edge to begin with. After deciding that there was no solution, the guests went on to enjoy their evening and the bartenders went on to complete their shifts, putting the incident behind them.

Having nearly forgotten this happened, months later, the seasoned bartender arrived at work again for her regular shift. It was a rather slow afternoon at first, and the evening happy hour hadn't quite begun yet. Above the rack of glasses behind the bar, there sits a couple shelves with the liquor bottles, normal to many bar establishments in their location, shelved for easy viewing and convenient bartender access. An array of whiskeys, vodkas, gins and more sit up on the shelves, prepared to serve many a thirsty customer. On that slow afternoon, one of the customers ordered his usual Tanqueray and tonic. The bartender provided him his drink and delicately placed the bottle back in its seat on the shelf. A couple minutes passed, and as she was chatting with her customer, there was a loud banging sound. They looked out the windows and around the restaurant, seeing nothing. It was almost like a car backfiring. Everything seemed steady. Moments later, in domino effect, the liquor bottles began to tumble off the shelves one after the other after the other. The bartender ducked for cover, and when the clamoring ended, she nervously peeked around her to see what mess had been made by the unseen force. Sure enough, every bottle was on the hard ground in front of her, but not one bottle was broken. Astonished and a little bit shaken up, she and some other staff began to clear up the mess. They simply could not determine what caused this. When the bartender finally reached to pick up the last bottle on the floor, she noticed it was the Tanqueray bottle she had utilized last before the liquor bottles came tumbling down. As she picked the bottle up, she couldn't believe her eyes. There was a single hole going through the top of the bottle, yet seemingly no liquid had spilled out. It almost appeared to be a bullet hole. What could possibly have left that? There was definitely no explanation for that anomaly. Some local rumors theorize that prior to the factory being erected on the land a community square had once sat there and public executions could have taken place right there in the village square. Could that be true and some sort of spirit be visiting from that dark time? Or was it simply a loud sound from residual times whose booming effect took it beyond the veil? There is much we can speculate, but one thing was certain: enough was enough, and the young barkeep and other staff were frightened. It was this event that inspired her to have a talk with her superiors, letting them know that working alone in the evening hours was just simply not an option.

The bartender at Voodoo Grill does not seem to be the sole employee experiencing unexplained occurrences while on her shift. Many of their staff members are no strangers to supernatural happenings around them at work. One such young woman, fairly new to the establishment, went to a closed-off area up the stairs to acquire some cleaning supplies at the end of her shift. She had just gotten back downstairs prepared to clean when she realized she had forgotten a single item, a bucket for the dirty mop water.

"Woops! I'll be right back," she called out to the staff members and scampered back up the steps. Suddenly, they heard a scream and ran to check on her. The new employee stood there gasping for air and pointing in front of her, unable to speak. Over a dozen cleaning buckets were spread out in an array in front of her as if waiting for her to come in and look for them. Even more astonishing, the Voodoo Grill management didn't even know they owned that many cleaning buckets and have no idea as to where they came from, let alone how they were displayed with such purpose. At least the spirit was proving helpful.

This young woman, however, did not appear impressed by her cleaning assistant and asked to not work any additional shifts alone either. At the Voodoo Grill, it seemed that the epidemic of frightened staff was spreading.

There is, however, one individual staff member who is not in a position to demand working with others. The primary hours of his shift are in the wee hours of the morning and require him to work completely on his own in the witching hours of the evening. His job is to provide maintenance and heavy cleaning for the establishment. A job description involving cleaning and handiwork that can't get done when the place is hopping with customers definitely takes some getting used to, as does any night shift or solitary work environment.

A seasoned New Englander, the maintenance man is familiar with historic buildings, creaks and sounds and the spookiness that these landmarks inherit. He admits that Factory Square and Voodoo Grill are no strangers to these types of occurrences, but only a few times has he been truly scared. He is one of the lucky—or I suppose *unlucky*—few who have gotten a peek behind the veil into that more elusive residual haunting. One evening as he was scrubbing down the bar area, he thought he saw something in the decorative mirror that was placed up against the wall and window area just behind the bar itself. The time was about 4:00 a.m. An uneasy feeling overcame him as if he was not alone. He looked up to the mirror to be sure of what he saw. The way the mirror faced toward him, depicting who would be sitting in the array of restaurant tables behind, would allow him to see if someone else was in the room. Upon looking into the mirror, the late-night employee caught sight of a group of men around a table. Naturally assuming that he had forgotten to lock the door, his instantaneous first reaction was to turn around and let the unassuming and possibly drunk visitors know that the bar was, in fact, closed. When he turned around to the bar tables, however, they were empty, with no evidence of visitors anywhere. The room was oddly still and quiet enough that you could hear a pin drop. The maintenance man turned to look in the mirror once more and, sure enough, saw the group of men still there. This time, he noticed that they were dressed in factory workers' attire that seemed to be dated around the 1920s or '30s era, he guessed. Still thinking perhaps he was tired and didn't see the guests, he whipped around to again inform them that the bar was closed. Just as was the result the first time, the bar tables were still empty, with no evidence of any drunk customers or swift-moving visitors. Finally, a third time, he looked again at the mirror and saw nothing but his own reflection. Deciding to shake off the incident since he had his shift to finish, the staff member proceeded to scrub down the bar. A peaceful night was not in the cards for him, though. Suddenly, the radio turned on and started playing big band jazz music typical of the 1920s. The employee was naturally most startled and alarmed by the sightings and music. Thinking the night couldn't get any weirder, he proceeded toward the radio to turn it off. When he did turn the radio off, wondering when the Voodoo Grill started playing such music in the first place, the music still continued to play. The power button clearly displayed the off setting. That would have been enough to scare most people, employee or not, right out of the building, but not him. He was not going to let this spirit activity get the best of him, despite how frightening it was. He then unplugged the radio. Expecting silence, once more he was met with alarm. Even unplugged, the music still blared out. The man walked away from the radio, trying to get his wits about him, and after several minutes, the music stopped playing. Not wanting to jeopardize his job, the maintenance man bravely finished his shift and chocked it up to just another New England haunting.

Their night-shift employee continues to burn the midnight oil at Voodoo Grill to the present day, explaining that small things happen all the time, such as footsteps, movements and especially the ringing of the kitchen bell. Often when the kitchen bell tolls, a chef can be heard proclaiming, "Order up!" at 4:00 a.m. It would seem that the ghosts have a sense of humor. Not one to encourage their antics, however, the diligent employee goes about his business and shakes his head. Paying them attention would just make it worse, and for now, all seems to be quite well with the spirits and the maintenance man being well aware of and accepting of one another.

Apparitions of factory workers and unexplainable activity are not centered on just the Voodoo Grill portion of Factory Square, despite how aptly named it may be. The entire factory was once a bustling hub for working and activity, thus it stands to reason that it is still a bustling hub for paranormal activity in all its facets and buildings.

Margherita's Restaurant, in the building just off Water Street and located on the second floor, has had its share of occurrences to include bar stools falling off the bar in unison, footsteps walking around toward the bathroom in the quiet of the night, unsightly apparitions and even a mysterious levitating fork, which some staff members were lucky enough to capture photographic evidence of.

Other testimonials to Factory Square's haunting nature come from condominium residents. During a ghost tour, one young man and a couple family members exiting an apartment caught wind of the spooky tales. They quietly stood behind and listened as I told the tales of the Voodoo Grill and the haunts of Factory Square. After I completed the summation, the curious watchers spoke with my husband, who had accompanied the tour, ready to divulge their own pertinent story. The young man said that he moved into Factory Square just a few months prior and had also been seeing apparitions of a man appearing in 1920s factory clothing, just standing and walking through his apartment, having no knowledge that the young man seemed to be living there. It seemed yet more proof of a residual haunting. The phantom factory worker just passing through seemed to have no sense at all that he had just walked through an apartment.

Factory Square continues to change its haunting type at every turn, proving its duplicitous abilities. Another resident has told a story of a haunting in her two-story condo, which she had always felt quite comfortable in. She had recently gone on vacation, and after a late flight, she was very tired. After arriving home from the airport, she went straight up the stairs and into bed. Having crawled into bed, she plugged in her cellphone next to her and fell asleep. Quickly, she was awoken by a bright light shining from downstairs. Alarmed that someone may be in the house, the resident nudged her husband and said, "Go down there and find out what that is!" Grumbling and begrudging, he tottered down the stairs. From the bed, she had seen the lights turn off and heard him return to their bedside. "What was it?" she inquired curiously. Her husband replied, "Well, the television was turned on, and I did notice something weird." He continued, "It was playing a television program, but the cable box was turned off." They tried to brush it off as a power surge and went back to sleep. Clearly, it can be assessed that a residual haunting wouldn't lead to the turning on of a television set, so an active spirit it must have been. Factory Square seems to be an endless trove of unexplainable, paranormal treasures.

Those large brick buildings filling blocks of Water Street in downtown Mystic have seen their fair share of visitors, employees and now residents. Having been such an important part of Mystic, Connecticut society and economy during the Civil War era and beyond, it is truly a historical landmark that you don't want to let go unnoticed at first glance.

Next time you are having a bite to eat or enjoying a cocktail at a Factory Square establishment, be sure to keep your eyes wide open. Perhaps you may be one of the select few to get a sneak peek back in time at the factory in

Standard Machinery Company, site of Factory Square, circa 1925. *Photo from the Dickinson Collection, courtesy of the Mystic River Historical Society, Inc., Mystic, Connecticut.*

full-fledged working action and see the factory workers operating machinery long since extinct in the industrial world. Or you may just have a more mischievous spirit play a trick on you and have the sensation that the spirit is quite aware that you are there, gasping in surprise at its behavior. It is more than evident that all facets of the factory block on Water Street have come together to create a place bustling with paranormal activity. The lights are always flickering, strange items are hovering and sometimes an apparition will stroll by with leisure. Nothing seems impossible inside the brick-and-mortar walls of Factory Square.

Chapter 6

SPRIGHTLY CHILDREN, A WATCHFUL LADY AND THE ECLECTIC COLLECTION OF SPIRITS THAT FREQUENT THE FORMER EMPORIUM

15 WATER STREET

The building that sits at 15 Water Street in Downtown Mystic, presently owned and looked after by the respected Mystic Arts Center, harbors a paranormal receptivity in its very appearance. Though already a prominent feature on the haunted walking tour route, guests get an early glimpse of the establishment en route to the Captain Daniel Packer Inne just a little farther down the road. As we stroll by, I often see people point to the Water Street icon and whisper, "There must be something in that building" or "Do you see that place? It gives me the creeps" or "Miss, is there a spirit there? I can just feel it. Are we going to stop there?" Perhaps the brooding Italianate architecture gives the structure a foreboding ambience, or perhaps the ghostly energy is so dominant that it emanates from the floors, walls and windows themselves, grasping immediately the sensitivities of anyone nearby. Alternately, it could be the richness of the building and the land's history with such a variety of purpose and human energy over the past 150 years that creates such a sensation and warrants such a reaction. It seems that regardless of a person's historical interests, he or she can simply look at the building and feel importance in its antiquity. Better still is the probability that all these elements have come together and created the perfect storm for such an efficacious spiritual realm.

The history of the building remains a bit vague in some respects, but just enough of its multifaceted past has been documented or passed down in local oral history, allowing us to get a pretty fair assessment of where its ghostly residents came from. The building contains about 4,250 square feet throughout three stories. In the past, the first two stories have included a storefront and the third story an apartment. There is also a basement, but it isn't "finished," so to speak.

The history of this particular land plot begins before the creation of the infamous Italianate structure. We have already learned about the demise of the Pequots at the hand of British colonial settlers and neighboring tribes in the Mystic massacre, but Native American tribes warred with one another long before the arrival of Europeans. Southeastern Connecticut was no stranger to these disputes. Though the main fort was farther up the hill, there was an encampment or safe area for Pequots from their Narragansett enemies on the land where the building on 15 Water Street would be erected.

A general store was established on the land in 1713 after the area faced quite a population influx. The general store remained in operation for many years until it was taken down to make way for the current breathtaking structure. The former Emporium building was erected in 1859 by Isaac Randall and Dwight Ashby. Isaac Randall was well known in town and ran the cotton gin manufacturing plant across the street at one of Water's Street's fellow haunts, the former Reliance Machine Company at Factory Square. The Civil War would begin just two short years after the building's construction. From the get-go, the Emporium seemed to set up shop as another local general store and convenience store of sorts. As the 1860s roared and the Civil War raged throughout the country, the glorious new building on Water Street served as the Mystic Country's post office and war office. People could still take care of their mail deliveries and obtain basic needs from the general area of the store, but half of the building was a war office where young men would come and register for battle. Additionally, all news of death and injury for these Connecticut locals fighting for the Union would be delivered to the 15 Water Street building. Local women, children or older men not involved in the fighting themselves wanting to inquire on the well being of their husbands, sons, fathers and brothers would go to the building each day hoping for *no* news. Back then, no news truly was good news, for if a loved one's name wasn't delivered to the war office, the wives, mothers and children were to assume that, at the very least, that those they held dear had survived another day or week in a war filled with bloody battles.

The next one hundred years would be the time period when the history of the building gets a bit hazy and the truth of the matter is somewhat buried. From the latter part of the 1800s until the mid-1900s, the former war office wore many hats and served as a boardinghouse, several stores and, both arguably and scandalously, a brothel.

Though some locals insist that the building was a general store of sorts from its creation and did not possess such a colored past, there are other locals who have insisted that the building did indeed serve time as a brothel. Naturally, a brothel in Mystic would have been quite the source of controversy, since Mystic is and always has been a relatively small community. If there were a brothel at any point in the 1800s or early 1900s, many would have looked on it with reproach, and every resident would have known exactly which men frequented it. The men must have not seen this as a source of embarrassment or shame, for if it did exist, it existed long enough for there to be regular customers. The very existence is a distinct possibility since historically we know brothels have always existed in some sense throughout all societies. After many years as a more rigid, Puritan society it would seem Connecticut was likely not exempt from more scandalous activity. The exact timing remains arguable, and it is unclear whether the potential brothel was in the mid- to late 1800s or spanned into the 1900s.

The mysterious and hazy era of the 1880s up through the early 1900s gave tales of the other services that the building provided, even if only for a short while. One of these was as a boardinghouse. Early editions of the local New London newspaper the *Day* mention that there was a known boardinghouse on Water Street in Mystic. Though it is possible there was more than one boardinghouse on Water Street at the time, we may assume from local tales and newspaper evidence combined that this is likely in reference to the former Emporium. By description, the boardinghouse would have housed mostly summer guests, while a select few others may have stayed for a longer term. Adding yet more color to its varied past as a true renaissance building of multiple purposes, research also revealed that 15 Water Street had a brief stint as both an apartment building and even at one time a restaurant. A structure of multifaceted talents it could be called, indeed!

The first owners to name the building the Emporium were Mr. Lee Howard and Mr. Paul White. After they purchased the building during the Vietnam War era, they did some major restorations and eventually opened for business in 1965. Prior to their store, that particular landscape of Water Street was far from hustling and bustling with popular activity. Some in the community had even seen Water Street as a slum and described it as such. Resurrecting the building on 15 Water Street brought new life and a sense of flair back to Water Street that had long since been forgotten.

Mr. Howard and Mr. White became known for their merchandise of rare antique items, knick-knacks and penny candy. The first floor maintained a construction of floorboards made from ships that were in the Mystic River

15 Water Street before the Emporium, circa 1959. *Photo courtesy of the Mystic River Historical Society, Inc., Mystic, Connecticut.*

in the 1700s and 1800s. These floorboards were one of the only structural elements that escaped damage from yet another Mystic conflagration that tried to decimate and ravage the entire Italianate Victorian structure in 1976. Though the first floor escaped relatively unscathed, the second and third floors, along with a majority of the merchandise, would not find themselves so lucky, and they were virtually sitting in complete destruction. Adding fuel to the fire, so to speak, was the fact that no rational reason could be found for the destruction. There was no terrible storm or electric shortage that could be blamed during the investigation. After thorough examination, it was deemed that the fire was of suspicious origin.

Though after the fire Howard and White had hopes to open the building within a month, they encountered some major setbacks. The renovations and repairs took a toll, both financially and emotionally. After two years burdened by these stressors and coming to terms with the inability to reclaim treasures lost (including items that were originally placed at President Lincoln's inauguration), Howard and White had begun to contemplate selling their pride and joy but pressed forward. Sixteen dumptrucks of trash, a full rewiring, replumbing and significant sandblasting led the owners to finally be able to duplicate what the storefront had once been prior to the fire. For these two gentlemen, however, it would never be the same, and their time together with the Emporium had come to a close. It was time for them to sell. The building, though, still had so much life and history left within it, and Mystic was surely not ready to say good-bye. True, the fiery curse nearly claimed the glorious structure but the Emporium's spirit (maybe thanks to the spirits residing within its walls) was just too strong and the perfect buyers made themselves known.

In 1978, a pair of gentlemen with a flair for the unique and eccentric set their sights on the Emporium. These men were named Mr. Robert Bankel and Mr. Evan Nickles. Mr. Bankel, in fact, had a most unique tie to the building's history since his great-great-grandfather William E. Wheeler once owned the property sometime shortly after the Civil War. In Wheeler's retirement from being a sea captain, he took up selling dry goods at the prominent storefront and war office on Water Street (do remember—it remained a store for at least a short time before other ventures ensued). Nickles and Bankel, however, kept with the Howard and White theme of more quirky merchandise, selling everything from candy to costumes, postcards to games, books to clothing and small knick-knacks all the way

Entrance to the Emporium store, circa 1970. *Photo courtesy of the Mystic River Historical Society, Inc., Mystic, Connecticut.*

to valuable antiques. For thirty-five years, Nickles and Bankel remained as stewards of the building, in their own words, until it was time for them and the building to part ways for new chapters.

This decision was tough for Bankel and Nickles, and the Mystic community struggled to wrap their heads around it. However, their decision to sell the property led to the Mystic Arts Center's recent acquisition of the structure in the latter part of 2013. Though the building would no longer be called the Emporium, the Mystic Arts Center has allowed residents of Mystic to come up with a new name for the building as it readies itself to turn another page in the Water Street history books.

One thing is certain to remain steadfast and consistent throughout the changing of the hands, and that is the safe harbor this building seems to provide for so many ghostly inhabitants. These particular spirits are most certainly not liable to get up and leave merely because a new storefront or resident moves in. As long as the structure stands they seem to be happy within their home.

When strolling through Mystic, 15 Water Street seems to be the location where guests get the most chills, capture evidence of ghosts on their cameras and, on occasion, see full apparitions. It is the building that draws in everyone's psychic third eye, and admittedly, oftentimes when presenting at the Emporium, I myself am overcome with the sensation of dizziness and get my clothing tugged and often feel touched. It's as if the veil between the living and the dead is virtually nonexistent at that property. For intuitives, it's an overwhelming sensation, and even for those who don't claim to have paranormal sensitivities, the very essence of this building makes them feel as if they do. In fact, when at 15 Water Street, it would appear as if everyone is a sensitive, even if only for the brief time there.

Paranormal stories may have been told throughout the building's history, but the first traceable accounts date back to the 1960s, when Howard and White first purchased the property. While becoming acquainted with their new property, Howard and White realized the amount of work that would need to take place in order for the building to redevelop into a shop. It was evident that significant renovations were necessary. As they were going about renovations, they decided to initiate their work with some simple repairs. At the time, the floors on the second level weren't fantastic nor as exciting as the antiquated ship boards were on the first floor, but they would definitely be able to suffice after a good coat of paint. The men took turns painting one day, and later into the afternoon, one of the men remained to finish up painting one of the rooms. Looking down toward the end of his painting job, he noticed that he had painted himself into a corner, and feeling like a fool, he realized he would have to stand there for some time and watch the paint dry around him. As the new owner stood there cursing himself for not thinking his plan through, he heard what sounded like someone entering the building. Naturally, he assumed that it was an unwitting customer who preemptively assumed that the store was already open for business and had waltzed right in. The man was certain he had locked the front door, but since he had just painted himself into a corner, he thought, it stood to reason that his head was somewhere else that day and he had forgotten.

"I'm sorry, we're closed," he yelled so that his voice would tunnel downstairs. "Please join us when we open in a few weeks." The walking continued and sounded as if the visitor were in heels. The *clack, clack, clack* sound on the old shipboards that made up the floor eerily echoed from the first floor. *Hmmm*, he thought. Maybe she didn't hear him. He pondered and decided to yell down again to the woman who seemed to be wearing such very loud heels.

"We're closed. I need to ask you to please leave," he said. *There*, he thought. He had most definitely made himself quite clear now. However, the woman still continued to walk around in complete disregard of his statements. Suddenly, he heard her drawing nearer the stairs and not nearer the exit. Coming to the unfortunate realization that he was going to have to ruin his paint job and address this prospective customer in person he skidded around the outside of the room trying to damage as little paint as possible to reach the door. At this time the footsteps seemed to have ceased for a moment. He looked in the room next to him on the second floor, seeing nobody. Just then, the sound of footsteps suddenly resumed, and he heard the clacking high heels coming up the last step. Perhaps he hadn't seen the visitor. There are lots of nooks and crannies in old buildings, not always great for visibility, but this meant the trespasser was heading right for his new paint job. He approached the room he was just in, ready to find out who this audacious person was. The man peeked into the doorway, and sure enough, high heel prints trod all the way through the paint. He, in fact, saw them being formed before his very eyes. While he looked around the room, searching for the culprit, his heart beat faster as he realized that he saw no one. Then the new entrepreneur gasped, for the walking ceased inexplicably at the middle of a wall.

Not knowing what to make of what happened before his very eyes, the owner made the decision then and there to never paint over those footsteps and leave them as a testimony to all customers and visitors of the paranormal spirits that reside in the building. This particular spirit is often referred to as the "Lady Upstairs." That uncomfortable feeling that people get in the upstairs rooms, as if they're being watched, can often be attributed to her lurking about in unearthly form. Her presence emits strong sensations hard to get rid of for any visitor in the building. Unfortunately, the remarkable footprints were one of the many losses during the fiery incident in the 1970s that took almost the entirety of the second and third floors of the building. Because of this, the footsteps can no longer be seen by visitors today. The legend, however, will continue to be told throughout the seaside community.

The New England Spiritual Team, Inc., (NEST) was able to corroborate this tale, along with many others indicated by the locals. The New England Spiritual Team, Inc., is made up of paranormal investigators who have conducted investigations throughout the state of Connecticut, and one of their highlights includes a night spent inside the former Emporium, which allowed them to retrieve some intriguing evidence. During one of their overnight stays, they were capturing orbs on photograph when they heard footsteps, possibly even footsteps of high heels, walking above their heads on the second floor. The seasoned investigators all hushed quietly to make sure they weren't mistaking their own footsteps for those they heard. Sure enough, the footsteps continued, and their audio equipment was able to detect the sound clearly. Suddenly, Michael Carroll, one of the founders of the New England Spiritual Team, Inc., realized that they had forgotten one very large thing about the Emporium. The layout included a third floor that was an apartment where the manager of the storefront resided. The store manager was very supportive of the investigation, having experienced numerous occurrences of paranormal activity firsthand in the building that served as both her home and workplace for over twenty years. During the investigation, the ghost hunters called her on the phone and asked if she had been walking around. It was about 1:00 a.m. or so. She could have still been awake. The manager indicated on the call that she was indeed awake, but she was not walking around, and if for any reason she had gotten out of bed that night, she certainly was not wearing high heels. Eager to help the NEST team, the manager inquired if there was anything she could do. Michael Carroll replied that indeed there was. As part of their probe into the occurrence, they had to confirm that the sound they heard was paranormal and could not be debunked.

He then asked her if she could walk around so that they could at least determine their constant versus their variable. It was imperative they become familiar with the sound of her footsteps. If they could hear her walking about, they could at the very least become familiar with that sound. After they determined what it sounded like when she walked around the third floor, they could disregard that sound if it was picked up by their audio recorders.

The lady kindly obliged, and while they heard a slight creaking of boards when she walked around, the adept investigators could not hear her footsteps. They were certain what they did hear was NOT the sound that was previously emanating through the rooms and immediately drawing all of their attention. The footsteps continued off and on throughout the night. It sounded like high heels waltzing through sometimes, and other times it was more the sound of footsteps or scuffling about, perhaps that of children running around. Some photographs depicted orbs, and the crew members as a whole said they could just feel that strong sensation of paranormal residents from the spirit realm throughout their investigation.

The Lady Upstairs seems to monitor the building quite visibly, almost giving a sense that she knows all or at least knows all that's going on in her building. During one ghost tour, after I had completed my speaking at the location, a guest presented me with a curious inquiry. It was one of those evenings that the dizzy sensation had overcome me profoundly, and I had already known that the spirits were monitoring their visitors quite closely. The guest, a young lady in her teenage years inquired, "Is there still someone living upstairs now? I saw a lady looking down at us." It is next to impossible to see the third floor apartment on the sidewalk right up next to the building. More than that, the building had been completely vacant for some time and there was no one inside. The building had been sold and emptied of all merchandise at this time in November 2013. After being informed that the building was indeed vacant, the young woman continued, "No, it's not. I saw her in that window." She then pointed to the second floor—most specifically, the room where those footsteps had been heard—and provided more detail, saying, "I saw a lady with a tight bun in her hair kind of nodding her head up and down looking out at us. I thought she was just watching the tour." Everyone surrounding the young woman turned to look at her. Their faces were turning shades of pale, and they had goose bumps popping up on their arms. The revelation that they were in the presence of the Lady Upstairs overcame them. The tour participant had seen an apparition that very night of the high heel–clad woman who seemed to be guarding the premises with a wary eye.

Who the woman could be remains quite a mystery. Was she from the times of the brothel? Could her time spent there during such a time of scandal have become burned into the memory of the building, leading her to keep watch for prospective customers or perhaps a person of the law looking to shut down the operation? Perhaps she was from the war office era, a frequent visitor checking on the status of her loved one away in the Civil War, and now she is a Civil War widow waiting on her lost love to come. Whoever she may be, she is an active entity that perhaps isn't warmly received but has always made herself known.

The lady of the house is not the only one there, and while she spends most of her time upstairs on the second floor, the first floor has some more playful, sprightly and happy spiritual residents that have been witnessed so often they actually received names from some of the staff and visitors who have frequented the establishment over time. Throughout the years, staff members often received inquiries regarding two young boys who were always seen playing in the corridor, on the stairwell or among some of the children's toys, laughing and giggling to themselves and having a grand time. The customers and visitors would always ask, "Who are those two cute little boys playing around the store?" Pointing to their store associate, they'd press on, saying, "Are those your boys?" Some customers would describe

The building at 15 Water Street, site of the former Emporium, under renovation, circa 2014.

them and remark, "They are just adorable, but they're all covered in soot!" The commentary on the boys was always some variation of that comment. Initially, staff members would respond, bewildered as to what the customers were talking about. Sometimes they, too, thought that they could hear the giggling but dismissed it as in their head or as being an actual customer's child. When clients also started remarking on these sounds and visions, a red flag was raised. At first, the stunned staff would tell the customers that they didn't know what they were talking about. Of course, this alarmed everyone in the scenario, but after a while, the staff, managers and owners spoke and decided to give the boys names. This way they could refer to them fondly and without hesitation when customers inquired about their presence. They also jointly decided to brush them off as harmless spirit entities and to carry on without fear. The employees gave the ghostly boys the nicknames Willy and Billy. It's a bit silly, since this is the derivate of the same name, but it seemed to work out just fine and appease the masses. Then, when customers would walk in and say, "Who are those two cute little boys all covered in soot?" the cashier could simply respond, "Oh, that's just Willy and Billy. They love to come in and play." Goodness knows how many customers walked in and out having encountered Willy and Billy, never actually realizing that they'd seen spiritual apparitions with their own naked eye. History suggests that Willy and Billy may be the spirits of young boys who would have been hired to stoke fires in the winter months for small amounts of change. This could account for their soot-covered appearance and perhaps their cause of death, though we can never know for sure. Their presence coincides perfectly with the very elusive history of the building.

If you stand quite still, you may just feel a tug on your shirt and almost hear a giggle faintly behind you, but do not be alarmed. It's likely just Willy and Billy saying hello and appreciating your company.

Many people look into the windows during the dark hours of the night to see if they can be the ones lucky enough to catch a glimpse of the young boys themselves. Sometimes though they may not see them with their naked eye, their cameras have better luck. Indeed individuals have been able to pick up ghostly figures in the windows almost looking right back at them. On more than one occurrence, pictures have been taken in the windows on the first floor depicting the small outline of two little heads peeping outside at the cameras and visitors looking in. The pictures have displayed the outline of eyes, noses and mouths on the little heads, though any detailed facial features are not completely distinct. Others report that their cameras will only let them take pictures of the first floor; as soon as they try to take pictures of the second floor, their batteries die or their cameras shut down unexpectedly. Some speculate that spirits can take the energy from batteries and electronic devices to help manifest their own energy, and perhaps the spirits at the former Emporium establishment do just that.

With what can be known as "psychic photos," spirits can be captured at varying times in their attempt to appear. Sometimes it's a mere flash of light or an orb, and other times it's the shape of a human. A camera depiction of a full apparition is the rarest kind, and the photographic evidence captured of Willy and Billy—while not a full apparition—has at least gone one step above orb.

The building at 15 Water Street brings historical richness, multifaceted utilization and friendly and not-so-friendly spirits all in one Italianate Victorian structure to downtown Mystic. At your next stop to 15 Water Street, regardless of what business endeavors may be there over the years to come, be sure to keep an eye out for Willy and Billy, the Lady Upstairs and any other spirits that may try to grab your attention while you are there. Also remember to keep in mind that you do not need to be a spiritual sensitive or paranormal enthusiast to get a taste of the otherworldly action. The spirits there aren't shy, and sometimes the phases of the moon or your very personality are enough to bring them out of the woodwork.

Chapter 7

THE RETURNING GUESTS

ANTHONY J'S BISTRO AND THE ANCIENT MARINER RESTAURANT

Sometimes a ghostly sighting in Mystic can be a rather welcome experience. The ghostly apparition may also serve as a reminder of eras from the not-so-distant past. A couple local restaurants, in fact, tell tales that their frequent guests who had more or less become monuments to their favorite dining establishments before their passing may still be visiting. Staff members also claim to know just who those guests are.

Anthony J's Bistro, located on Holmes Street just past the intersection of East Main and Holmes, offers a renowned wine cellar and an array of Italian dishes perfect for a bistro ambience. The building, with beautifully gabled roofs and shingled sides of aged wood, gives 6 Holmes Street a warm and inviting look. The former homestead, which has served as a restaurant and residence in the recent past, was first erected in 1844 by a man named Daniel Patrick. Rumor has it that the house was not originally built on Holmes Street but slightly farther back from where it sits and then was subsequently moved at some point. It was possibly first located on Willow Street. Of all the fires that haunt that particular area of Mystic landscape, Anthony J's has remained untouched, and the structure is almost wholly intact from the time it was built. Much of the history regarding the building remains a mystery. Spanning 4,200 square feet, the building was originally made to be either a single-family residence or more likely a multi-family residence. Some local historians suggest that it may have been a food shop or some type of general store early on, but property records leave that difficult to confirm.

Postcard of Holmes Street, including the future site of Anthony J's, the second house on the left. *Image from the Stinson Collection, courtesy of the Mystic River Historical Society, Inc., Mystic, Connecticut.*

In the 1980s and early 1990s, the man who would open AJ's food store, which subsequently turned into Anthony J's (AJ's Restaurant), Anthony J. Torraca, fondly known as Skip, purchased the property, taking the first step in turning it into what it is today. Anthony and his partner, Debbie Gross, have maintained a consistently raved-about cuisine, and the restaurant remains a landmark dining establishment in the downtown community. Anthony J's Bistro is a revered local favorite for family gatherings and intimate dining out. The property is still split between residences and the restaurant. The visiting ghostly guest, however, can be found in the restaurant. Even as a ghost, this spirit seems to spend his visits and time among the wining and dining, just like he used to in life.

Over the thirty years that Skip has owned the restaurant, he has seen many clients come in regularly. As the years press on, many of his regular customers grow older and pass away. When this happens, Skip will often put pictures of them in his bar area to commemorate his revered guests, frequent customers and, most importantly, his friends.

One of these guests whose photo hangs up behind the bar was a man named Richard, more commonly known as Rich. Rich loved nearly everything about Anthony J's, including the ambience, the wine, the food and especially the staff, but there was one thing that bothered him. This was the holiday decor that Skip and his family utilized for the restaurant around the holiday season. Rich found the decor gaudy, tacky and just plain not to his liking. The decorations he rather despised were large ornamental balls of red, green and gold that are commonly strung from ceilings and around holiday trees near Christmas time. For some reason, this is what bothered poor Rich the most. There was nothing strange about the particular decor, but it definitely did not strike Rich's fancy, so he would always teasingly criticize Skip about it.

Despite Rich's joking comments and criticism, Skip and the management continued to use the large ornamental balls when December rolled around. One year, prior to the holidays, Rich sadly passed away. Time passed after the mourning of their friend, and it was time to prepare the restaurant for the festive season once more. The staff laughed a bit and smiled when they went to get their holiday decorations that year, remarking on how disappointed Rich would be in them still using those tacky ornaments. When they went to gather the decorations from their storage area in the basement, however, they noticed that one of the large ornamental balls that had hung in the main dining areas was not among the rest. Bewildered, they searched their homes and storage unit, still unable to locate the missing ornamental ball. Again, they laughed and chuckled, "Well, at least Richard would be getting his way somewhat this year. But really, where is that ball?"

When Skip, Debbie and the staff had long forgotten the incident and their missing ornament, confirmation and evidence surfaced suggesting that Richard was indeed making sure he got his way from the afterlife. It was a warm, humid, summer morning in mid-July when they unlocked the restaurant and prepared to open for a day of business. There was nothing remarkable about the day, and it seemed like any other—until they opened the front door and their eyes were drawn directly to the main dining area. There, sitting in the middle of the floor, was the large ornamental ball that had gone missing just about seven months prior. Seemingly out of nowhere, there it sat. Nothing else was amiss.

After letting out an audible gasp, they all whispered, "Richard," knowing that it had to have been him who was just popping in to say that he finally got his way removing those Christmas decorations, and clearly he picked July because he could safely know that his point had been made. There was simply no one else it could have been.

Anthony J's Bistro entrance sign, circa 2014. *Photo by Shelby McInvale.*

Richard seems to be a friendly spirit, likely just appearing to check on the holiday decor. Perhaps some of the other previous patrons whose photos line the wall come by to watch over and check in on their favorite dining establishment as well.

Some staff members believe that another ghost—perhaps not Richard—likes to come by in the quiet times of the restaurant or bar, particularly in the wee hours of the morning when they are closing up. The bartenders and servers sometimes have the sensation that someone is standing by them, watching them just closely enough to make their hair stand on end or give them goose bumps. Perhaps it's a spirit from the 150-year past of the building, such as a previous resident or someone who died in the home. We may never know who some of the spirits lurking around the wine cellar are, but if nothing else, they add a special character to the Anthony J's Bistro and just can't help but spend their time among the lively gatherings of locals that the establishment brings in.

These particular proprietors and owners, Torraca and Gross, must create quite a welcoming environment in their establishments for they also have returning guests at another local food place in town: Anthony J's sister restaurant, Ancient Mariner restaurant, quaintly placed on East Main Street just on the other side of the drawbridge. The nautically themed restaurant

West Main Street in Downtown Mystic, circa 1926. The Ancient Mariner site is at the far right. *Image from the Stinson Collection, courtesy of the Mystic River Historical Society, Inc., Mystic, Connecticut.*

sits among buildings that have suffered various fires, and the current structure was erected on a site where most recently a laundromat had stood. Prior to that, the property had served as varying storefronts.

The current Ancient Mariner's building was erected in 1974 and sits at just one story stretching back to the parking lot of the Steamboat Inn. The Ancient Mariner boasts varying surf-and-turf menus, plus a raved-about bar area. Decoratively, Ancient Mariner gives a taste of the seafaring heyday of Mystic's past with pieces from old historic ships and six hundred oars from all kinds of boats, both antique and modern, lining the walls throughout.

Historically, the structure does not date back too far, but it does date back in restaurant years plenty long enough to have obtained some regular customers and to be a popular place for friends to gather. Owner Skip had a dear friend named John who was a federal agent his entire life. After his retirement, John was absolutely thrilled to find that his friend had established a new pub in his home area of Mystic. After a career in law enforcement, John had developed a fairly morbid yet witty sense of humor, which his friends were always laughing recipients of. He would come into the restaurant and joke with Skip and the others that when he died, he would come in and haunt the restaurant. They would laugh and joke back, "Oh, don't say things like that," but he would reiterate that it would indeed happen and then sit back and enjoy his time at the bar. Unfortunately, after years of his fun times at the restaurant, John suddenly passed away of a heart attack. True to his word, though, he did not yet abandon his second home at Ancient Mariner.

The owners hung a picture of John in the restaurant close to his favorite barstool in memoriam of their dear friend and tried to operate the restaurant without any hiccups in light of their recent loss. Not long after his passing, they came in one morning to open the restaurant and noticed his photo was a little bit askew and a couple of the six hundred oars lining the wall were turned upside down. *Hmmm*, they thought. *That's odd*. This had never happened before, but they proceeded to secure the oars and the photo, proceeding with business as usual.

Everything remained quiet until a couple days later. When the owners came in once more to open the restaurant, John's photo was once again askew and three different oars were turned upside down. They had to wonder if this was no longer a coincidence but actually a sign from their departed friend that he was indeed coming back to haunt them in their restaurant and playing his fun-loving tricks to prove it.

The Ancient Mariner Restaurant, circa 2014. *Photo by Shelby McInvale.*

As if to give the owners and staff the confirmation they required to know for sure that it was their friend, yet another defining incident occurred. That very evening, a very telling object moved on its own. When the staff went to close the restaurant, they turned down all the lights, stacked up all the chairs, wiped down the tables and the bar and finally stacked the barstools on the bar. Everything was routine as usual. As they headed toward the door to depart, the owners, who happened to be the staff members closing that night, felt compelled to take one last look around the restaurant. As their eyes scanned the premise, one thing immediately caught their eye. The barstool seated by John's photograph, his favorite barstool where he always sat when he came to enjoy the food and drink, had reseated itself. It happened almost as if to say, "Yes, it has been me that has been moving the oars and the photo. I told you I was going to haunt the place. I'm not quite ready to leave you guys just yet."

Instead of being scared, both Skip and his partner Debbie smiled because they knew the haunted happenings were from their dear friend and he had never left them at all. He would always be watching over his close acquaintances and his favorite Mystic cuisine.

Current reports indicate that inanimate objects continue to move throughout the restaurants, be it holiday ornaments like at Anthony J's or just some dinnerware. The windows also seem to open and close themselves regardless of the weather and not due to any waitstaff or other employee's chore-like duties. Whenever these things happen, or an oar tips over, there always seems to be the confirming evening ritual of that one barstool reseating itself at the bar. It's a welcome validation that it's still their dear friend up to his tricks, keeping his promise and spending his time in a place he loved so very much.

A community full of New England history has its full share of spirits spanning decades. However, a lively, friendly community full of close family and comrades can also bring the spirits of loved ones who are watching over and checking in on their loved ones. Mystic has its fair share of those friendly spirits as well. This is evidenced by dear Richard at Anthony J's and the lifetime friend John at Ancient Mariner. Unlike many of the other haunted establishments in Mystic, the staff members at these restaurants rarely if ever fear working alone. Even at Ancient Mariner, those who work at the bar into the wee hours of the morning have an overwhelming sense of calm. What better spirit to have watching over you than a man who protected others as a career federal agent in his life who just enjoys a good prank on his friends?

As you walk around Mystic, remember to embrace the spirits, both old and new, of all generations past, for they all are surely walking among you.

Chapter 8

LEGENDS AND FOLKLORE
OF THE MYSTIC RIVER

STRANGE HAPPENINGS AND UNEXPLAINED
SIGHTINGS THROUGHOUT MYSTIC COUNTRY

The telling of legends and tales, along with the passing down of stories around the crackling flames of a campfire in the dead of night, are a tradition that can be traced back through many generations of our ancestors. As centuries have passed, tales have been told of creature-like beings, such as Bigfoot, or sea monsters like Nessie of Loch Ness to all those who dare walk alone in the woods or swim in mysterious depths of lakes by themselves. Throughout the globe, sightings of galloping unicorns, full-moon werewolves and blood-thirsty vampires make people step back and wonder at the very possibility that just perhaps there is really an existence of things beyond our wildest dreams or nightmares. All of these are but a small sampling of the legends that surround us. New England is home to many of its own fables, chock-full of inexplicable and mystical beings wandering among us yet seen only by a select few. They include sightings of something one may have only imagined when reading a fantasy novel, yet suddenly there they appear before your very eyes. Visions and encounters with the unexplained have no boundaries. No matter how skeptical or pragmatic you may think you are, it could be you for whom the legend comes to life. Some of these tales are ones of good luck and fortune. Others bring with them an omen, a sign of bad luck or perhaps a strict warning to heed.

Seafaring, oceanfront or riverside communities' stories can often bring their own unique set of nautical legends and nightmares. The ocean is full of its own secrets, remaining such a mystery not just to all of us beach goers but to science as well. The seas have been ravaged by very real pirates and sharks or whales larger than ships. Shipwrecks are often unearthed or sometimes even drowned cities, creating a ghost land and keeping history alive in their unexplored depths. There are also tales of ocean dwellers never proven to be real in science yet written of by those who spent their lives on the sea, giving us legends of krakens, mermaids and other unbelievable sea creatures.

Seaside communities often report tales of boats or ships that seem to float lifelessly down the river, almost as if indicating their wish to dock locally. Often there appear to be no crew members, and on the occasions there are human forms, they materialize as no more than faceless shadows on the boat. With Mystic's rich history of fishermen, whaling and industrial shipping industry, it will come as no surprise that the small southeastern Connecticut community has some ghost ship tales of its own.

Some reports tell of a ship that departs the Mystic Seaport and heads slowly in the direction of the Mystic River Drawbridge. As it rolls toward the bridge, residents and tourists see the historic ship and become awestruck. They notice quickly that it's not the Seaport's world-renowned *Charles W. Morgan*, the last of an American wooden whaling fleet dating back to 1841. What they see could not be a whaling ship due its small size, but it definitely dates back to the 1800s in appearance. No one appears to be manning the ship in one version, and there are no crew members to be seen anywhere. Whether the weather is gloomy, grey skied and rainy or clear blue skies with the sun illuminating and reflecting off the glistening ripples on the water, the ship feels comfortable making its eerie appearance.

This 1920 postcard shows the Mystic River Bascule Bridge (Drawbridge). *Photo courtesy of the Mystic River Historical Society, Inc., Mystic, Connecticut.*

The Mystic River Drawbridge, manned by an operator, always opens for oncoming vessels, no matter their size. Lights and bells go off around the bridge indicating that it will indeed lift the passageway up into a ninety-degree angle. Vehicles come to a halt at the blinking red lights, giving plenty of room. The bridge gracefully opens, and the boat passes through. When this particular mysterious vessel approaches the bridge from the Seaport, however, the bridge does not let out any indicators that it will be open. In fact, it seems as if the bridge has absolutely no indication of the approaching ship whatsoever. Concerned citizens and visitors look onward and discuss whether they should call the authorities in fear that there might be some horrible type of accident.

As they prepare to contact the police or the drawbridge operator, they look back once more out their windows or standing on the sidewalk and notice that the mysterious vessel, manned by no visible bodies, has disappeared before their very eyes. There is no wake in the water behind where the ship was just seen and no indication that it was actually there. Shocked, those who saw it whisper to one another, "Where did it go?" Had their eyes deceived them? No one knows for sure which boat this was or if it was one lost at sea 150 years ago, taken over by pirates or caught in a storm and never able to reach its Mystic home. Perhaps for the past decade and a half, the vessel is still attempting to gain safe harbor, stuck in a never-ending tale of woe.

Compiler and editor of *A Mystic River Anthology*, Judith Hicks, tells tales of another ghost ship in the local Mystic River waters that was only seen on rare occasions by travelers, passersby and local residents. This ship would specifically appear just as the shadow of night fell upon the town. This ship floated, not sailed, down the river, yet it seemed to quietly make progress and gain momentum with its purposeful flow. The air would be still, almost so calm that it brought a strange ambience of its own, with no wind or even a breeze to aid any vessel traveling the river waters. Unlike the first ship, a dark figure can be seen out of the corner of your eyes standing at the front of the ship, almost indicating that he would be the ship's captain. No sounds are heard, and the man appears motionless. The ship halts briefly and then resumes floating down the river before it disappears once more. Legend has it that the ship is coming home to bring back one of its own crew who met his fateful end while out on the unpredictable sea.

To be sure, not all of Mystic's legends are ghostly in nature, yet they are still quite mysterious and indicative of some sort of supernatural presence.

In the Northeast, there are residents who may be familiar with tales of a Pigman whose first documentation dates to the early 1970s in Northfield,

View of Gravel Street, circa 2014. *Photo by Shelby McInvale.*

Vermont. A North Country folklorist told a tale of a creature that traumatized and frightened some local classmates of his nearly to death shortly after they departed a school dance to wander off into the local woods and have a party of their own. The teens decided to hang out by a sandpit close to a community cemetery. It had become the perfect hiding place to indulge in some underage drinking and not get caught. Suddenly, the young men returned toward the school, beside themselves with fear. Crying, shaking, trembling and almost unable to speak, they finally managed to utter to their classmates what they had seen. The boys claimed that they witnessed a mutated-looking man, almost appearing as if half pig, kicking around sand on the hill above the sandpit. As they inched a bit closer to peer at the monstrosity, they recognized cloven prints in the sand nearer to them, only attributable to swine. Tales continued throughout the small Vermont community afterward about this five- or six-foot-tall man with beady eyes, a pig snout and some hair covering his whole body. Reports surfaced that he would be seen rattling in garbage cans or coming in the night to steal dogs and cats. Over time, incidents quieted down, though sightings of a frightening, hungry Pigman evolved and spread throughout the region and into the neighboring states.

Connecticut has tales of Pigmen, but one of the most frightening may come from Mystic. Local Mystic residents have told tales of what they call the Mystic Pigman. Similar to the incident in Northfield, the first and most alarming sighting of the Pigman was by young high school boys. The local Mystic boys went to high school in the late 1970s and early '80s and at that time were known as punks and bullies by their classmates. Due to their reputation, the story coming from their mouths seemed to have an extra ring of truth and veracity to it. After all, why would the young boys who picked on weirder people be the first to tell such a compelling supernatural tale?

The young men reported that one evening as they were walking down Holmes Street in Mystic, they heard a young woman screaming. When they heard her cries for help, they immediately headed closer to the river, where the screams were coming from. Horrifyingly, the lads lay their eyes on what appeared to be a man throwing the screaming woman into the water as if to drown her. Thinking they had arrived in plenty of time, the boys started shouting and screaming at the man to stop what he was doing, saying that they would call the police from a local shop. It was at this point that the man threw the woman under the water, and she did not resurface. The boys gasped in inconceivable awe. The man then turned to look at the young men, who were no longer such tough guys but scared little boys trembling in their sneakers. As he looked at them, the man snorted and made swine-like vocal sounds out of what appeared to be a pig-like face. The pig-man creature then dove into the water where he had thrown the woman and also did not resurface. Pale-faced, the boys told their classmates the story in gory detail and thus the legend of the Mystic Pigman became very real, scaring residents, visitors and schoolchildren alike. It was indeed reported that a local woman had gone missing shortly before this incident, and her case remains open. Some can't help but wonder if this inhuman creature from beyond had anything to do with her disappearance. The case of the Pigman as an entity of its own also remains unsolved.

The menacing and possibly evil Pigman is not the only mythical creature local teens have reported seeing around the community. In fact, in the more recent years, the Stonington Police Department has been receiving calls stating that a faun or satyr has been running around by the Mystic River and through local properties. After a brief glimpse, the faun disappears, and the police have found no evidence regarding its sightings. Naturally, the assumption was that this was a prank devised by the local teens, but the calls have continued, and many of the callers indicate desperation, genuine concern or confusion in their tone. For those unfamiliar with the term, a faun or satyr is most commonly known as a half-man, half-goat and can often be found in ancient Greek and Roman mythological stories.

A Pigman and a real faun both reside in such a quaint seaside community? It may sound far-fetched, but to those who have seen such things, their sightings remain very real, and they regard their vivid observations as proof that supernatural beings may still walk among us.

Mysteries of Mystic are not limited to the recent past or to mythical creatures. There may have been murders in the riverside locale that were never solved. Perhaps such morbid mysteries aid in the development of supernatural creatures and ghosts in the area. Local newspaper reports actually reveal an incident involving the discovery of human remains under the streets of Mystic. At first, this would make sense, knowing that the bodies from the Mystic Massacre were likely spread throughout the land. However, coroners and other experts of the times believe that this was not the case with the human bones found on Stonington Road in October 1915. Newspaper headlines began with the title "Found Skeleton of Large Man" and continued as follows:

> *While digging…on the Stonington Road Friday afternoon laborers in the employ of the Vito Construction Co. unearthed the skeleton of a man about a foot and a half underground. One of the men's picks crushed through the skull, but most of the skeleton was intact. The opinion seems to be that rather than an Indian it may have been the skeleton of a man who had been put out of the way in a hurry—or if the plain, awful truth must be told a murder victim!...How long they have been there is impossible to say.*

Mystic's journey of darker and ominous legends is, of course, ongoing and tales of Mystic past show supernatural creatures, murderous mysteries, nautical anomalies and sometimes ominous events bringing an element of foreboding. Some of these darker incidents brought that unfortunate sense of foreboding to local women who had their betrothed and other loved ones at sea. Their unfortunate sightings would be enough to make anyone's skin crawl and your heart patter with worry.

In one example, the aforementioned local Mystic anthology also tells of a woman who experienced a most unimaginable loss after a dreadful sight appeared during her wedding planning with family and friends. The sighting revealed the fate of her loved one before it was even confirmed.

In September 1875, as autumn rolled into southeastern Connecticut, the leaves had begun to change into their vibrant shades of red, orange, yellow

A 1930s postcard of scenic Gravel Street, downtown Mystic, Connecticut. *Photo courtesy of the Mystic River Historical Society, Inc., Mystic, Connecticut.*

and gold. It had been a stormy year, and as the seasons changed, many weather disturbances and ferocious winds seemed to surround the local area. On one of these stormy, rainy evenings, young Lydia Palmer took advantage of the time with her family members to plan her upcoming nuptials to her fiancé, a fisherman out at sea. The fire was roaring, and all was safe and warm inside their home except for the wandering raindrop which made its way down the chimney quickly extinguished by the fire. As Lydia sat there among her loved ones, she began to stare at the window in a kind of daydream when, in a swift start, she let out a blood-curdling scream. Complete horror shone in her eyes as she began to almost hyperventilate and cry. She pointed at the window, unable to speak for some time. As Lydia pointed at the window, her engagement ring pointedly fell off her finger, actually shattering in two pieces as it hit the ground. In the windows panes depicted clearly for her and the family to see was the face of Lydia's fiancé. His face appeared grisly, grim and almost a shade of pale green, indicative that he had died or was to die at sea.

Wishing that this omen was wrong and that whoever sent this image to her brought false news, Lydia tried to brush off the incident. Lamentably, this false sense of hope did not last long, for the very next morning, news was delivered to her door that her fiancé and another fisherman had gotten caught in the awful storm at sea while they were so close yet so far from home. He had been washed overboard the *Commodore* and drowned. Whether her fiancé appeared grisly and grim, as if he were visiting her from beyond the grave, or whether it was an omen delivered from some other spiritual entity remains unclear. What is not unclear, however, is that the omen was correct, and poor Lydia became the almost-widow of the Mystic community area for years to come.

As a quiet seaside community, Mystic is filled with legendary tales of its own. Be it a murderous creature with a swine-like appearance or mythical sightings of fauns and satyrs walking among us, you just never know what you may bear witness to. As you stroll about the town, you may hear tales of murder victims' bones strewn under the street or ghostly ominous sightings of the seafaring men who would never make it home. Perhaps as you next walk over the drawbridge, you may catch a glimpse of the floating vessel just before it vanishes.

Mystical in name and mystical in happenings, the beautiful downtown landscape of the aptly named Mystic has a world of tales just beyond the veil. As the sun sets over the Mystic Country, be aware of all that surrounds you. There are ghosts of generations pasts, unseemly monsters, ravaging fires that seem to spark on their own and an entire world that we can't always see. History comes alive as the moon rises over the downtown streets, and the flowing river water reminds everyone who trod on the ground that mysticism truly lies within Mystic Country.

BIBLIOGRAPHY

Books

Cave, Alfred. *The Pequot War*. Amherst: University of Massachusetts Press, 1996.

Fought, Leigh. *A History of Mystic, Connecticut: From Pequot Village to Tourist Town*. Charleston, SC: The History Press, 2007.

Greenhalgh, Kathleen. *A History of Old Mystic, 1600–1999*. Old Mystic, CT: The Indian and Colonial Research Center Archives, n.d.

Hicks, Judith, ed. *A Mystic River Anthology*. Wickford, RI: Dutch Island Press, 1988.

Keeler, Charles Carroll. *The Packer Homestead & the Captain Daniel Packer Inne*. Mystic, CT: Mystic River Historical Society Archives, 2007.

Mason, John. *A Brief History of the Pequot War: Especially of the Memorable Taking of Their Fort at Mistick in Connecticut*. Boston: S. Kneeland & T. Green, 1736.

Mystic River Historical Society. *Mystic, CT: Images of America*. Charleston, SC: Arcadia Publishing, 2004.

Old Mystic Walking Tour. Mystic, CT: Mystic, Indian and Colonial Research Center Archives, n.d.

Whitehall and Its Restoration. Stonington, CT: Stonington Historical Society, 1970.

ARTICLES

Eldredge, Charles. Personal Scrapbook. January 27, 1930.

Green, Judy. "The Mystery of The Missing Bell." *Mystic River Press*, April 28, 2005.

Hicks, Judy. "Destruction, Disasters & Demolitions–Mystic's 350th Anniversary Walking Tour Commentary." Mystic River Historical Society Archives, 2004.

Howard, Lee. "A Mystic Institution for Sale." *The Day*, July 1, 2012.

Kimball, Carol. "Of Whitehall and Other Old Burial Grounds." *The Day*, February 27, 1997.

Levitt, Alice. "Local Legends." *Seven Days*, October 28, 2009.

New London (CT) Day. "Blaze Ravages Store in Mystic." September 2, 1976.

———. "Factory Tract Sold to Builder." March 24, 1973.

———. "Found Skeleton of a Large Man." October 16, 1915.

———. "Mystic Fire One of Many." January 2, 1975.

———. "Mystic's Firebug Causes Damage of $40,000 Today." October 11, 1910.

Noyd, Deborah. "Memories Linger at the Emporium." *New London (CT) Day*, September 3, 1977.

"Old Mystic Schools in Bygone Days." N.d.

Underhill, John. "A New and Experimental Discovery of New England Containing: A True Revelation of Their War-like Proceedings These Two Years Last Past with a Figure of the Indian Fort or Palizado." *News from America* (London), 1638.

ELECTRONIC SOURCES

Connecticut History on the Web. "Readings: The Pequot War." http://www.connhistory.org/peq_rdgs.htm.

Connecticuthistory.org. "Pequot War." http://connecticuthistory.org/topics-page/pequot-war/.

The Mashantucket (Western) Pequot Tribal Nation. "The Pequot War." http://www.mashantucket.com/pequotwar.aspx.

Old Mystic Inn. "History of the 1784 House—The Main House at the Old Mystic Inn." http://www.oldmysticinn.com/history.htm.

VIDEO OR DVD

Ten Days that Unexpectedly Changed America: Part 1. DVD. Directed by Jeffrey Friedman, Barak Goodman, David Heilbroner, James Moll and Bruce Sinofsky. The History Channel, 2006.

ABOUT THE AUTHOR

Courtney McInvale is a Connecticut native, born and raised in a real-life haunted house in East Hampton. Her childhood home was investigated by the Warren family during her teenage years. Since then, she has always been attracted to the paranormal and has acquired a unique sensitivity to spirit activity through her experiences. Though Courtney may have established a lifelong propensity to experience true ghostly occurrences and hauntings, she absolutely loved growing up in colonial, historic New England and wouldn't have had it any other way. Living in Connecticut, Courtney inevitably obtained a great passion for history, legends, local lore and, oddly enough, politics. Courtney took these passions and headed off to study international relations at Catholic University of America in Washington, D.C., where she obtained her bachelor's degree. While pursuing her degree, she spent a semester abroad growing well acquainted with her Irish ancestry and falling even more in love with the study of history. Wanting to honor her own family history, McInvale even married abroad in the Emerald Isle to her husband, a fellow Connecticut native and history aficionado. Professionally, Courtney has spent time working for various departments of the federal government in both D.C. and Vermont before migrating back to her home state of Connecticut, where she opened up Seaside Shadows Haunted Walking Tours. Seaside Shadows is a local tour featuring tales of ghosts and spirits throughout Mystic, Connecticut. Courtney makes history come alive with true tales of spooks and is aspiring to expand her paranormal business in the coming years. Ms. McInvale is absolutely ecstatic to be pursuing her passions of writing, history and paranormal investigation, all within her beloved New England. Courtney resides in eastern Connecticut with her loving husband, Marty, who also shares her fascination with supernatural phenomena. When Courtney and Marty aren't chasing ghosts and giving tours, they can be found spending time with their small family of furry animals, including dog Danny Boy and cats Lennon (after John Lennon) and Lovebug.

Visit us at
www.historypress.net
....
This title is also available as an e-book